ORGANIZATIONAL ASSESSMENT

A FRAMEWORK FOR IMPROVING PERFORMANCE

Charles Lusthaus, Marie-Hélène Adrien, Gary Anderson,
Fred Carden and George Plinio Montalván

Inter-American Development Bank
Washington, D.C.

**International Development
Research Centre**
Ottawa, Canada

2002

Published jointly by the
International Development Research Centre
PO Box 8500, Ottawa, ON, Canada K1G 3H9
http://www.idrc.ca
and the
Inter-American Development Bank
1300 New York Avenue, N.W.
Washington, D.C. 20577, USA
http://www.iadb.org

© 2002 International Development Research Centre/Inter-American Development Bank

National Library of Canada cataloguing in publication data

Main entry under title :

Organizational assessment: a framework for improving performance

Co-published by the Inter-American Development Bank.
Includes bibliographical references.
ISBN 0-88936-998-4

1. Organizational effectiveness : Evaluation.
2. Sustainable development : Developing countries.
I. Lusthaus, Charles.
II. Inter-American Development Bank.
III. International Development Research Centre (Canada)

HD58.9O73 2002   658.1   C2002-980096-X

This publication may be read and ordered online at the IDRC Booktíque,
http://www.idrc.ca/booktique and at http://www.iadb.org/pub
To order by e-mail, contact: idb-books@iadb.org or order@idrc.ca

Contents

Chapter Three
CAPACITY 41

Chapter Four
ORGANIZATIONAL MOTIVATION

Chapter Seven
IMPLEMENTING AN ORGANIZATIONAL ASSESSMENT

Foreword

The field of international development mirrors the complex ways in which the people of the world rely on each other to survive and flourish. The framework in this book probes the inter-reliance within, and between, organizations in developing countries. Within these organizations, people and groups of people act with, and depend on, each other to reach worthy common goals. On a larger scale but for the same reason, these organizations themselves must learn to collaborate effectively. This book focuses on the importance of organizations to development and provides a framework to help them operate more efficiently.

How do we make development assistance more effective and efficient? We have progressed greatly after several decades of change and reform. Yet the pace of economic and social change for which we can accept some credit still falls short of the need, and of its potential. For development organizations, changing ourselves to heighten our own performance is a critical part of widening and deepening our reach. Supporting myriad government ministries, research centers and executing agencies in their quest for better performance also remains a major challenge. We continue, too, to face our boards' and donor governments' desires for accountability and for results. Rightly, they want to know that our support for a project will assure that it brings sustainable improvements, whether that support comprises loans and grants, or whether it boosts research and research capacity.

What, then, can agencies like the International Development Research Centre (IDRC) and the Inter-American Development Bank (IDB) do? What frameworks can help guide our actions and help us learn for the future? We need economic and social changes. To attain these, we know that organizational behavior must change, too. Our own experiences show that organizations worldwide must learn to work better together to reinforce each other's accomplishments. Those of us who give them development assistance and loans play a role in fostering that synergy and cooperation.

This book arose from the need to give organizations concrete ways to study their own critical interplay and to change them, for the good of the entity and its goals. The book contains a set of usable, tested tools that organizations can employ to change themselves, so that they can better change the world.

IDRC first published this framework in 1995. The IDB very quickly became involved in applying and using it, and has been instrumental in the field-testing. This greatly updated and expanded framework has grown from our combined experiences. IDRC and Universalia have applied these tools in organizations in West Africa, South Asia, and, along with the IDB, in Latin America. Each organization has its own story to tell. This book interprets these stories so that others can learn and benefit from these experiences.

As with the first book, this new edition reports on external and internal efforts to strengthen organizations, using concrete actions based on clear-eyed diagnoses at the onset of development activities. To use the book and benefit from it, you only need be interested in improving your organization's performance—whether you are in a new organization, an organization in change, a joint venture, or an "electronic organization."

The book itself has resulted from the kind of collaboration we seek to foster among organizations in the development community. The IDB has helped update many of the theoretical and practical components, and is pleased to help disseminate them further. The mutual learning we have experienced as we have co-published this book lays the foundation for further interagency cooperation.

Work in developing countries—in fact, in all countries the world over—is always a work in progress. Seldom can we stamp the development process as "finished." *Organizational Assessment: A Framework for Improving Performance* is also a work in progress. As collaborators in researching, testing and writing it, we realize that when it comes to the task of changing organizations, few solutions are absolute. For that reason, we urge you to send us your feedback and comments. We know we'll write subsequent editions, and we welcome your contributions.

Nohra Rey de Marulanda
Manager, Integration and
Regional Programs Department
Inter-American Development Bank

Terry Smutylo
Director, Evaluation Unit
International Development
Research Centre

Preface

The roots of this book go back to 1993, when we began to write our first book about improving the performance of research institutions in developing countries (Lusthaus et al., 1995). Development agencies have found it difficult to make adequate and useful investments aimed at improving the performance of research centers. Since we were working on this issue, the International Development Research Centre (IDRC) asked us to share our experience in written form with the wider development community. Almost 10 years later, we have a much wider set of experiences under our belts, and at the same time institutions and organizations matter now more than ever. There continues to be a need to invest in organizations in the developing world in systematic ways that can significantly improve performance over both the short and medium terms. As we began to discuss the development of this text, we asked Fred Carden and George Plinio Montalván to join our team and add their experience and insight.

In this book, we take the organization as the basic unit of analysis, considering it to be a social unit that has an impact on our day-to-day lives. Culture and language play a crucial role in understanding the functioning of organizations around the world. In our dialogue with developing countries, we have come to realize the various levels of complexity involved in carrying out organizational assessments in these countries. To overcome this complexity, organizations must develop a common framework and concepts whenever they engage in organizational assessments. We have found that the framework and concepts in this book help to make such assessments successful.

Organizational Assessment: A Framework for Improving Performance puts forth a framework for analyzing the strengths and weaknesses of an organization in relation to its performance. The text introduces a heuristic framework that has guided our work for the past decade or so. In general, the framework posits that organizational performance is a function of its enabling environment, capacity and organizational motivation. It goes into a great deal of detail in trying to capture the ideas and concepts that underpin each of the four broad organizational ideas (performance, environment, capacity and motivation). In this framework, organizational performance is seen as a result of the organization's work.

Unlike our first edition, published by the IDRC in 1995, this book adopts a more generic approach toward organizations and is not primarily focused on research centers and nongovernmental organizations. Over the past decade, we have been privileged to work with a wide variety of government ministries and agencies, not-for-profit organizations, international organizations and financial institutions, and private sector firms. Thus, we have expanded the experiences for which the framework has been used, changed some of our analytical constructs, and revised our concepts in order for the framework to be more applicable to a wide range of organizational types.

This book is written for organizational practitioners. By this we mean organizational leaders and consultants who are interested in better understanding the present state of organizations and how to choose areas for investment that can improve organizational performance. At a very basic level, we are interested in working with colleagues who see improving organizational performance as an important piece of the puzzle that defines development effectiveness. We see organizational performance as an area that has been neglected by the development community. In this context, we want to open a dialog with those organizational practicners who feel that systematic analysis can be used to support the process of organizational learning and change. Beyond the general assessment framework, the book provides methodological tools and support for those interested in using it as a template for carrying out organizational assessments.

All organizations—whether for-profit or not-for-profit, government or civil society, or privately or publicly owned—engage in some form (formal, informal) of organizational assessment. What is not agreed upon are the frameworks, methods and processes that have proven to be successful in informing stakeholders about the status of the organization. Is the organization performing well? Why or why not? This book is designed to add to the theory and practice of organizational assessment.

During the years that we have worked on this project, we have benefited greatly from the many colleagues, clients and friends who have discussed various ideas with us and critiqued our work. It is a long list that starts with our own organizations and extends well beyond them to the literally hundreds of organizations with which we have worked or had contact over the past decade. All of them have contributed in one way or another to this book. Unfortunately, they are too numerous to mention.

We would also like to acknowledge the contribution made by Diane Eyre, who did the initial editing. Valerie Chalhoub, Tracy Wallis, Mark Pestinger and Maroushka Kanywani deserve special mention for putting in the finishing touches. Finally, we would like to thank our families for their unfailing support.

Charles Lusthaus,
for the authors

Chapter One

INTRODUCTION: CHANGES IN DEVELOPMENT ASSISTANCE

One might wonder why, over the past 22 years, six Nobel prizes have been awarded to scholars who specialized in delving into the world of institutions and organizations. What is so special about institutions and organizations to garner this kind of attention and accolades? Are they the key determinants of economic, social and political progress? We believe they are that—and more. In fact, we believe that the inability of development agencies to understand and change the performance of the organizations and institutions with which they interact has significantly impeded progress in many developing countries.

Healthy and vibrant organizations are an essential ingredient for a nation's development. All nations have a dizzying array of large, small, powerful, onerous, disciplined, flexible and competitive political and economic organizations. Some perform well, others less well, and some fail altogether.

Organizations vary in a number of ways (Aldrich, 1999). Legislative chambers, political parties, government agencies, the judiciary, private firms, trade unions, nongovernmental organizations (NGOs), schools and parent-teacher associations— all are "organizations." An organization is made up of people working together toward a shared goal. Organizational goals differentiate organizations from other social collectives such as families. Although organizations have goals, however, their members might feel indifferent toward the goals, or may be alienated from them. Because organizations are made up of people, many of their activities are designed within the limits of the organizational members.

One of the frustrations of organizations is the inability to match existing membership with the activities the organization knows it should be carrying out. Also, organizations have distinct boundaries. People know who is inside and who is outside the organization. Membership has privileges. Organizations attempt to specify rights and responsibilities, codes of behavior, value systems, rituals, power and power relationships, and leadership. Organizational rules and their enforcement govern organizations and create the organizational "culture." Organizations and the societies within which they operate both create rules and are governed by these rules. Finally, organizations are socially constructed, and their success or failure is governed by this interaction.

Overall, organizations are important social units of many shapes and sizes that play an integral role in our day-to-day lives. These social units have evolved from small families and gatherings of people, to large government entities (communities, states, nations, the United Nations) and private enterprises (small and medium-sized businesses, national and global enterprises). Civil society agencies are also evolving from local community groups into global agencies. Today, a wide range of organizations is required to carry out increasingly complex and adaptive tasks that, in turn, respond to an increasingly complex environment.

As organizations evolve and try to succeed, they adapt to their environment and to technical developments. This often leads to increased specializations of functions, people and infrastructure. As organizations specialize their functions and the infrastructure required to maintain and carry out those functions, they require greater interdependence with the various work groups. In other words, specialization increases complexity.

Organizations are not only composed of individuals, but also interdependent groups with different immediate goals (derived from specialization), different ways of working, different formal training, and even different personality types. People who work in accounting departments often have very different personalities, goals, training and styles of work and socialization than do people who work in advertising or marketing departments (Meyers and Briggs, 1980).

Different departments also have their own work processes and flow. Each organizational unit has its way of carrying out work based on its goals and understanding of the appropriate technology required to meet its goals. Over the past two decades, computers have dramatically changed how many organizational groups carry out their functions and coordinate with other groups.

The way an organization transforms its resources into results through work processes is what people call "systems." These systems are subject to all sorts of influence from within and outside the organization. Today's organizations are "open systems"—that is, they are constantly both influenced by and trying to influence external forces.

In this dynamic context—the institutional environment—organizations and the groups that comprise them are constantly trying to adapt, survive, perform and influence. Sometimes they succeed, and sometimes they do not. The question then becomes, how can organizations better understand what to change and influence to improve their ability to perform? Systematic diagnosis is an important part of this process, and there are many ways to conduct such an organizational examination. The purpose of this book is to provide development practitioners with a systematic framework or approach to better understand organizational performance and to pinpoint the elements that significantly affect that performance.

Over the last ten years, we developed a framework of institutional and organizational assessment that culminated in the book entitled *Institutional Assessment: A Framework for Strengthening Organizational Capacity* (Lusthaus, Anderson and Murphy, 1995). The book is also available in French, *Évaluation Institutionelle: Cadre pour le renforcement des organisations partenaires du* CRDI (Adrien, Anderson, Lusthaus and Murphy, 1996). We tested the use of the framework in a range of organizations in the developing world, which resulted in a second book entitled *Enhancing Organizational Performance: A Toolbox for Self-Assessment* (Lusthaus, Adrien, Anderson and Carden, 1999). We found that a systematic framework provides a common language, and is helpful to better understand how and where to intervene to improve performance (Lusthaus, Adrien and Perstinger, 1999).

As the framework evolved, it gave us a basis for discussion and comparison across regions and organizations and development problems (Lusthaus, Anderson and Adrien, 1997). The framework presented in this book supports an organizational diagnosis. It is an update of our earlier work that focused primarily on research institutions. More recently, we began to work with international executing agencies involved in seeking loans from international financial institutions (IFIs). These agencies are trying to use bank loans as investments to improve their ability to serve their countries and constituencies.

Over the years, the framework became a tool in its own evolution as it helped us to continually refine our thinking and to continue learning. In other words, the framework is not a finished product, nor do we want it to be. This approach to assessment is flexible enough to be valuable to a wide range of practitioners in a wide range of environments.

PURPOSE

We had three goals in mind when we began to write this text. First, we wanted to write about organizations and their importance to development discourse. Unlike our first edition, we wanted to write about a wide variety of organizational types, rather than just research centers or organizations involved in development research. Organizations are fascinating to us—they come in all sizes and shapes. Yet, development theorists seriously overlook them. We have tried to provide a wide assortment of organizational examples. The framework is put forth as generic, useful to all organizations and individuals interested in organizational diagnosis.

Second, we wanted to update our earlier work. While our framework is still basically the same, there are several important new areas that were changed or adapted. For example, we expanded our idea of performance to include a factor called financial viability. We did this because of our experiences with both governmental and nongovernmental agencies that were increasingly being asked to compete in market-like conditions. In other words, for the first time, these organizations needed to build their capacity to raise funds. In the section on performance, we also added information about balancing the various performance factors. Again, this insight is drawn from both the theoretical work of the "balance scorecard" (Kaplan and Norton, 1996), as well as the practical realization that organizations need to constantly satisfy competing performance expectations.

Third, we wanted to make the topic of organizational assessment accessible to practitioners. Over the past five years, we worked with a wide assortment of organizational practitioners interested in both organizational and social change. They know that while money helps change, it is how the money is used that makes a difference. And they recognize that financing directed toward strengthening the capacity of organizations is good for development. Furthermore, practitioners realize that they need to better understand the forces that affect the ability of organizations to persist in efforts that may lead to a change in performance. An increasing number of practitioners need to learn more about organizations and how to change the level of their performance.

OVERVIEW

Early management theories assumed that organizations existed to serve a purpose (Etzioni, 1964), and that the role of management was to support this purpose by strategically gathering and applying resources in an efficient manner. However, experience showed that organizations did not serve a singular goal, but rather had multiple goals and sub-goals (Quinn and Rohrbaugh, 1983). Some of these supported the original organizational purpose, while others did not.

Furthermore, in practice, an organization's goals were constantly and easily displaced (Selznick, 1957). Time changed people's perceptions of the goals, leaders altered the goals, and organizational events caused a shift in priorities or even systems. Structures sometimes inadvertently acted as a counter-productive force, and inhibited the achievement of objectives. Given this complexity, how were organizations and their constituents to know if they were moving in the right direction? How were they to measure performance and the factors associated with good performance?

Caplow (1976) argued that "every organization has work to do in the real world and some way of measuring how well that work is done." His conception of organizational performance was based on common sense, and on the notion that organizations need a way to concretely identify their purpose and assess how well they are doing in relation to it. This constituted an organization's institutional definition of its own purpose.

Since it was clear that organizations that did not make money went out of business, private firms used the common sense concept of profit as a way to judge their performance. Thus, at the simplest level, measuring financial growth was a way of assessing how "well" work was being done. Profit is indeed a significant and valid aspect of good performance, and many managers in the private sector used profitability as a complete metaphor for understanding organizational performance, and began to define their purpose, above all, in terms of monetary gain. In government and non-profit organizations, however, ideas about what constitutes good performance were not as clear. Schools help children learn and power companies supply electricity, but whether a root concept such as profit is an appropriate way to define good performance by those institutions was uncertain.

The adoption of profitability as a primary objective in the private sector was congruent with prevailing ideologies shaping management practices at the time. Management theorists in the early part of the century focused on devising scientific or engineering methods to increase financial gain (Taylor, 1947). In support of such management objectives, organizational assessment focused on identifying ways to improve the efficiency of workers. By "engineering" optimal ways for people to behave in specific organizational production systems, managers aimed to produce more goods for less money, thereby increasing profits.

Starting in the 1940s, more abstract and generic conceptions of performance began to emerge in the discourse on organizational performance (Likert, 1957). Gradually, concepts such as effectiveness, efficiency and employee morale gained ground in the management literature and, by the 1960s, were considered major components of performance (Campbell, 1970). Managers understood an organization to be performing well if it achieved its intended goals (effectiveness) and used relatively few resources in doing so (efficiency).[1] In this context, profit became just one of several indicators of performance. The implicit goal shaping most definitions of organizational performance was the ability to survive. From this perspective, an effective yet inefficient organization would not survive any better than an efficient organization that was not achieving its stated goals. Thus, prevailing organizational theories expected performing organizations to both meet their goals and to do so within reasonable resource parameters (Campbell, 1970).

Gradually, it became clear that organizational assessment and diagnosis needed to go beyond the scientific measurement of work and work methods (Levinson, 1972). The presence and contribution of those doing the work—people—emerged as yet another important organizational component to be factored into the performance equation. The conceptualization of people as an organizational resource gained ground as well. As a result, approaches appeared that aimed at shedding light on the potential impact of human resources on organizational performance.

For example, Rensis Likert pioneered the use of survey methods to diagnose organizations. Likert's theory assumes that participatory management practices lead to higher organizational performance. In this context, surveys were used to capture data on employee perceptions of a variety of organizational management practices such as leadership, communication and decision-making.

During the 1950s and early 1960s, the search for a significant variable that would lend diagnostic insight into the functioning of organizations led to the analysis of organizational structure as well. At the time, some believed that the most efficient organizational form was bureaucracy (Weber, 1947), and that consequently, organizations needed to diagnose how bureaucratic they were. The assumption was that the more bureaucratic the organization, the better performing and efficient it would be. Managers started describing government and private sector organizations in terms that operationalized Weber's criteria for bureaucracy—specialization, formalization and hierarchy—and emphasized bureaucratic components when diagnosing organizations (Blau and Scott, 1962; Hickson and Pugh, 1995).

Until then, organizational assessments had focused primarily on work, people (and their processes), and organizational structure. However, by the mid-1960s and into the 1970s, organizations in the public, for-profit and non-profit sector began to

---

[1] At the time, "morale" was still considered to be a component of broader efficiency indicators.

explore new ways to understand their performance. A range of alternative means of gauging performance emerged as a result (Steers, 1975). The assumption that there were only a limited number of standards of measurement (e.g., profits) was dismissed as more multivariate approaches were taken. New attempts were made to identify and examine the factors associated with high levels of performance. Organizational assessment was gradually becoming more complex and holistic, attempting to integrate as many aspects of an organization as possible (Levinson, 1972).

In the process of looking for better ways to understand and assess organizations, business and systems analysts created a variety of concrete cost accounting tools and techniques for helping managers understand financial performance. These included planning program budgeting systems and zero-based budgeting. Similarly, social scientists began to explore the different human and interpersonal factors that can influence organizational performance, such as problem solving, teamwork, morale, communication, innovation and adaptation.

As a result of these evolving efforts to analyze organizational success, several core practices to enhance performance emerged in the late 1970s and early 1980s. In turn, these gave rise to further approaches to diagnosing organizations (Kilmann and Kilmann, 1989). By exploring organizational aspects other than effectiveness and efficiency, practitioners began to recognize the importance of stakeholders— clients, staff, customers and suppliers—in the performance equation (Peters and Waterman, 1982; Walton, 1986). By the 1990s, ways to describe organizational performance and the factors associated with it in the governmental, private and non-profit sectors were clearly more holistic and comprehensive (Harrison, 1987; Osborne and Gaebler, 1992; Scott and Meyer, 1994). Today, as the 21st century begins, there is renewed interest in the role of social capital in terms of organizations and organizing (UBC, 1998). A few years into the new century, once again we find that "organizations do matter" (Savedoff, 1998).

EVOLUTION OF THE FRAMEWORK

At the start of our discussions on the framework, one of the important issues needing clarification was the definition of the unit of analysis. In the past, most assessment models focused on projects supported by organizations that either funded or made loans to developing countries or their agencies. Our interests were not project-oriented. Rather, we were interested in organizations and the institutional environment in which they operate (see Chapter Two). On the whole, the framework reflected a change in focus from how well the organization did its programming work, to how well it was performing as an organization within its particular institutional environment.

As we reflected on our experience, developed our ideas, and reviewed the literature, we concluded that the framework needed to be organizationally based (the unit of analysis) and focused on a systematic review of the factors that affect organizational performance. There was a massive amount of literature[2] and a wide assortment of ideas and concepts regarding the fields of management, organizational assessment and change. We felt that our framework needed to be broad enough to include many of the ideas from these fields.

Four insights guided the development and evolution of the framework. First, we recognized the complexity of the concept of organizational performance. After conducting more than 100 organizational studies and reviewing analyses done for the International Development Research Centre and the Inter-American Development Bank, we were struck by the small number of studies that actually described how well organizations supported by funding or loan granting agencies were doing "organizationally." Our colleagues in the private sector clearly have paid more attention to this issue, and use a wide range of measures to assess organizational performance (Kaplan and Norton, 1996). While this is changing some organizations,[3] diagnostic work carried out by development agencies and development banks does not produce data bases that would help benchmark organizational performance within key functional organizational groups across the world.

The second insight came as a result of the work of institutional economists (North, 1994). While our previous work included a review of the organizational context or environment, this review was mostly descriptive, geared primarily to providing background or contextual information. North's work, among others, provided a theoretical perspective for understanding the organization's environment. From our perspective, an important insight is that organizations both influence and are influenced by their environment. Government agencies and ministries make the formal rules, and are influenced as well by both formal and informal rules. They also enforce or do not enforce the rules. We are increasingly incorporating ideas related to both formal and informal "rules of the game" into the framework. Rules and their enforce-

---

[2] See our jointly sponsored Web site on organizational self-assessment that includes a searchable bibliography of over 2,000 citations. This can be accessed at www.Universalia.com.

[3] For example, our work with the Federation of Canadian Municipalities includes using benchmarked performance indicators to assess municipal performance.

ment play a critical role in the success or failure of organizations. In response, the organizational assessment framework places more emphasis than previously on assessing the environment.

The third insight emerged from admitting that it was often baffling why some organizations did so well despite operating under harsh conditions, with few resources and poor management systems. Such constraints notwithstanding, such organizations seem to use their resources wisely, accomplish a lot of work, and exhibit a relatively high level of organizational performance. We noticed that the staff and all those working with such organizations (clients, members, etc.) were remarkably motivated and greatly committed. Despite poor systems and conditions, they clearly believed in what they were doing, used all their ingenuity to create positive results, and were able to grow, prosper and learn how to adapt to changing circumstances. It thus became evident that organizational motivation was a factor worth exploring when doing an assessment. Yet, very few organizations actually understand this issue.

Finally, our framework was influenced by the work of those trying to understand organizational capacity development.

These insights, along with the experience gained during our previous work assessing organizational systems and capacity, helped shape the framework. In brief, the framework encompasses the following areas:

- Measuring organizational performance
- Understanding the organization's external environment
- Determining organizational motivation
- Examining organizational capacity

The schematic representation of the framework defines performance in terms of effectiveness (mission fulfillment), efficiency, and ongoing relevance (the extent to which the organization adapts to changing conditions in its environment). The framework implies that certain contextual forces drive performance: organizational capacity, forces in its external environment, and internal motivation. A brief explanation of the framework follows.

Organizational Performance

Three ideas capture the performance of most of the organizations with which we worked. First, most non-profit organizations view their performance in terms of how

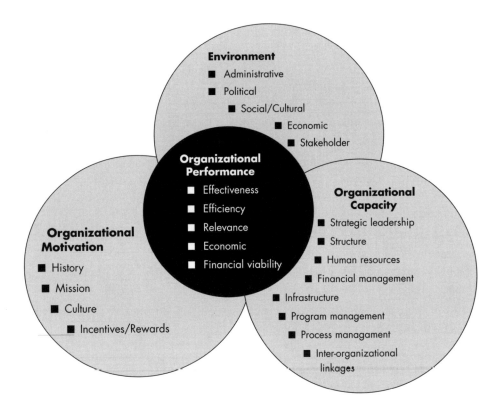

Environment
- Administrative
- Political
- Social/Cultural
- Economic
- Stakeholder

Organizational Performance
- Effectiveness
- Efficiency
- Relevance
- Economic
- Financial viability

Organizational Capacity
- Strategic leadership
- Structure
- Human resources
- Financial management
- Infrastructure
- Program management
- Process managament
- Inter-organizational linkages

Organizational Motivation
- History
- Mission
- Culture
- Incentives/Rewards

well they meet the mandates of their stated mission, purpose or goals. For example, a university is considered effective to the extent that it provides teaching, engages in research, and offers a service to the community. Nevertheless, universities, like other organizations, need to carry out their activities within some resource parameters.

To perform well, even educational organizations must operate efficiently, as measured, for example, by the cost per university graduate. As mentioned earlier, effectiveness and efficiency were at one time the standard concepts used for determining organizational performance. However, since the 1970s, many other variables associated with organizational performance have emerged, including morale, innovation, turnover, adaptability and orientation to change. Many new ideas are in circulation, and it is clear that different stakeholders want different types of organizational performance. Many of these ideas relate to ensuring that the organization is able to survive over time. This can be referred to as the "ongoing relevance to stakeholders."Our framework defines an organization as a good performer when it balance effectiveness, efficiency and relevance while being financially viable.

Organizational Capacity

Organizational capacity is the ability of an organization to use its resources to perform. If the organization itself is the unit of analysis, all of the resources, systems and processes that organizations develop to support them in their work can be assessed. An examination of the systems and management practices associated with human, financial and infrastructure resources helps provide insight into the use of organizational resources.

Within our framework, strategic leadership involves the strategies and niche management by the leaders that set the direction for the organization. Program management looks at the ability of the organization to carry out its institutional role, while process management examines the way the organization manages its human relations and work-related interactions. Structure identifies the links between how an organization is governed and its mission, as well as the roles that human resources and finance play in the organization's day-to-day activities. Finally, the framework describes the ability of the organization to manage its external relationships as "inter-institutional linkages."

Organizational Motivation

As stated earlier, we were inspired by several organizations that performed well despite having few resources and relatively undeveloped organizational capacities. Organizational motivation represents the underlying personality of the organization. It is what drives the members of the organization to perform. In our framework, we assess organizational motivation by analyzing a number of organizational dimensions.

One dimension we examine is organizational evolution and history—that is, how and why the organization got started, what its milestones are, and so forth. In a similar way, the assessment framework explores the organization's mission, values and vision in order to understand the driving forces behind it. The culture operating within an organization, and the incentives it offers, contribute to organizational motivation. Taken together, these factors give the organization its personality and affect its performance and quality of work.

External Environment

Organizations are open systems, and the external environment in which they operate is very important. Organizations need support from their environment if they are to survive and perform well. The environment is the key factor in determining the level of available resources and the ease with which an organization can carry out its activities. For example, poor macroeconomic policies lead to high interest rates, fluctuating currencies, and a host of conditions that make it difficult for some organizations to perform well.

The characteristics and quality of the environment—such as poor infrastructure in terms of roads, electricity and phone lines—can also hinder performance. Thus, in assessing an organization, attention must be paid to economic, political, sociocultural, environmental, demographic and technological conditions.

DEFINITIONS

The worlds of organizational and institutional theory, like any discipline, have their own language. We have put together a small glossary at the end of this book for those not familiar with this language. However, immediate clarification is needed for a few terms that are used here rather frequently and whose meanings are often confused.

Sector – An area under analysis, such as health, education, manufacturing, households or business. Sectors are made up of institutions and organizations.

Institution – The formal and informal rules by which system actors interact. Institutions involve a range of areas such as normative structures, culture, legal frameworks, policies and trends.

Organization – Formalized entities that involve a cluster of people who are brought together for a common purpose. Organizations both conform to and influence institutions. They include a wide spectrum of human activity and can be categorized as private or public, for-profit or non-profit, governmental or nongovernmental, and so forth.

Project – A planned undertaking designed to achieve certain specific objectives within a given budget and a specified period of time.

Program – A group of related projects, services and activities directed to the achievement of specific goals.

ORGANIZATION OF THE BOOK

This book has seven chapters, each dealing with a particular aspect of organizational assessment. This first chapter has highlighted the changes that have occurred in development assistance, one of which is the requirement for aid agencies to compete in market-like conditions. In addition, it has provided a brief historical overview of how thinking has evolved as regards organizations and their performance. There has been a shift from focusing primarily on work, people and organizational structure to recognizing the importance of staff, customers, stakeholders and clients. In sum, today there is a more holistic approach to assessing organizational performance.

Chapter Two places the organization within its context, that is, its environment. There is an inextricable link between an organization and its surrounding environment, which in turn affects how the organization performs, what it produces, and how it operates. The chapter provides a detailed review of the impact of formal rules, institutional ethos (informal rules), and capabilities.

Chapter Three deals with the eight components of organizational capacity. These include the various organizational and technical abilities that allow the organization as well as groups and individuals at any level to carry out functions and thereby achieve their development objectives. The chapter explores such issues as leadership, infrastructure, human resources and process management.

Chapter Four deals with the rather enigmatic aspect of organizations—that is, the forces that drive them to excel, commonly referred to as motivation. What factors explain the zeal with which some people do their work? The chapter explores four manifestations of organizational motivation: history, mission, culture and incentive/reward systems. It also looks at how these forces may be at work at different points of an organization's history.

Chapter Five deals with perhaps the most fundamental component of the organizational assessment process: performance. Traditionally, performance was defined by evaluating only an organization's effectiveness and efficiency, but this has shifted to include ongoing relevance to stakeholders as well as financial viability. The organization and its leaders must have good data on organizational performance and be able to understand the performance tradeoffs required.

Chapter Six explores methodological issues involved in carrying out organizational assessments, and emphasizes the importance of assessment to an organization and to those who have stakes in it. The chapter is not a prescription but rather an orientation as to what needs to be considered for effective organizational assessment.

The final chapter delves into the issues surrounding implementation of organizational assessment. These include ownership, ceremonial assessments, logic models and project traps. It also looks at how lessons learned can lead to improved organizational performance.

QUICK GUIDE FOR

ORGANIZATIONAL ASSESSMENT

This guide is intended to provide a framework for rapid organizational assessment during brief (one to two day) visits to an organization.

The guide provides some key concepts to reflect on as you analyze the organization's enabling environment, motivation, capacity and performance. Use these concepts in writing your organizational assessment report.

DATA SOURCES

Think about your data needs as your visit progresses. In the assessment process, attempt to:

❑ *Meet a suitable spectrum of stakeholders*
- Ministry and government officials
- Clients, beneficiaries
- Other donors, IFI representatives
- Relevant program managers/directors/administrators
- Human resources and IT managers/directors
- Researchers/teachers/other technical personnel
- Clients/stakeholders/organizational representatives
- Support staff

❑ *Observe relevant facilities*
- Buildings/grounds
- Project sites
- Teaching areas, libraries/document centers, laboratories
- Information systems

❑ *Observe the dynamics among people*
- Nature of meetings with you (who attends, who presides, etc.)
- Levels of participation and involvement of staff
- Processes for teaching and learning
- Nature of dealings with organization's clients
- How work is conducted; dominant paradigm
- Attitudes towards monitoring and evaluation

THE ENABLING ENVIRONMENT

Organizations do not exist in a vacuum. Each organization is set in a particular environment that provides multiple contexts that affect the organization and its performance. Characterize the organization's enabling environment using the following guidelines:

❑ *Describe and assess the formal rules within which the organization operates:*
- Legal framework
- Intellectual property rights
- Mandate
- Labor rights

❑ *Describe the institutional ethos within which the organization operates:*
- National evolution
- Cultural values
- Norms
- Taboos
- Religious beliefs

❑ *Describe the capabilities within which the organization operates:*
- Environment
- Labor market
- Economy
- Technology
- Geography

What is the impact of these environmental forces on the mission, performance and capacity of the organization? In what ways is the environment friendly or hostile? What are the major opportunities and risks resulting from the environment?

ORGANIZATIONAL CAPACITY

Organizational capacity underlies an organization's performance. Capacity is understood as the eight interrelated areas detailed below. Characterize the organizational capacity using these conceptual guidelines.

❑ *Assess the strengths and weaknesses of strategic leadership in the organization:*
- Leadership (managing culture, setting direction, supporting resource development, ensuring tasks are done)
- Strategic planning (scanning environment, developing tactics to attain objectives, goals, mission)
- Niche management (area of expertise, uniqueness, recognition of uniqueness)

❑ *Assess the strengths and weaknesses of financial management:*
- Financial planning (operating expenses, forecast future monetary needs and requirements)
- Financial accountability (rules for member use of financial resources, transparent/verified system)

❑ *Assess the strengths and weaknesses of the organizational structure within the organization:*
- Governance (legal framework, decision-making process, methods for setting direction, external links)
- Operational (roles and responsibilities, coordination of labor, coordination of systems)

❑ *Assess the strengths and weaknesses of the organizational infrastructure:*
- Facilities management (adequate lighting, clean water, electricity)
- Technology management (equipment, information systems, hardware/software, library)

❑ Assess the strengths and weaknesses of the following systems, processes or dimensions of human resources:

● Planning (recruiting, selecting, staffing, orienting)
● Developing (performance management, monitoring, evaluation)
● Career management (career development, training)
● Maintenance (health/safety issues, gender issues, quality of working life)

❑ Assess the strengths and weaknesses of the program and service management:

● Planning (identifying needs, setting objectives, costing alternatives, developing evaluation systems)
● Implementing (adherence to schedules, coordination of activities)
● Monitoring (projects/programs, systems for evaluating progress, communicating feedback to stakeholders)

❑ Assess the strengths and weaknesses of process management within the organization:

● Problem-solving (defining problems, gathering data)
● Decision-making (creating alternatives, deciding on solutions, monitoring decisions)
● Communications (exchanging accurate/vital information, achieving shared understanding among organizational members)
● Monitoring and evaluation (generating data, tracking progress, utilizing information, changing and improving the organization)

❑ Assess the strengths and weaknesses of inter-organizational linkages:

● Networks (type, nature, appropriate membership, utility, coordination, cost-benefit)
● Partnerships (type, nature, sustainability)
● Electronic linkages (communication networks, information equipment, information resources, people of all skills/backgrounds)

How does the organizational capacity affect organizational performance? What are the overall strengths and weaknesses of organizational capacity?

ORGANIZATIONAL MOTIVATION

No two organizations are alike. Each has a distinct history, vision and mission, culture, and incentive and reward system. Characterize the level of organizational motivation as determined by the following components:

❑ *Analyze the organization's history*:
- Date and process of founding
- Major awards/achievements
- Major struggles
- Changes in size, program, leadership

❑ *Understand the organization's culture*:
- Attitudes about working
- Attitudes about colleagues, clients or stakeholders
- Values, beliefs
- Underlying organizational norms that guide the organization

❑ *Understand the organization's mission*:
- Evolution of mission statement
- Organizational goals
- Role of mission in shaping the organization, giving it purpose and direction
- Articulating research/research products that are valued

❑ *Understand the organization's incentive/reward system*:
- Key factors, values, motivations to promote productivity
- Intellectual freedom, stimulation, autonomy
- Remuneration, grant access, opportunity for advancement
- Peer recognition, prestige

How does motivation affect organizational performance? In what ways do the history, mission, culture and incentive system positively and negatively influence the organization?

Organizational Performance

Every organization should attempt to meet its goals with an acceptable outlay of resources while ensuring sustainability over the long term. "Good performance" means the work is done effectively and efficiently and remains relevant to the stakeholders. Characterize organizational performance by answering the following questions:

❏ *How effective is the organization in moving toward the fulfillment of its mission?*
- Effectiveness of major programs (major achievements, levels of increase of literacy, miles of new roads, percent of girls obtaining education, new employment, level of research productivity, level of community health—areas directly linked to organization's mission and function)
- Effectiveness in meeting client expectations (internal and external clients served, quality of services/products)
- Effectiveness in meeting functional responsibilities—e.g., education (coverage, student achievement)
- Effectiveness in providing useful services (delivery of services to clients/beneficiaries, research community, technology transfer)

❏ *How effective is the organization in fulfilling its mission?*
- Cost of products and services—benchmarked comparisons, if possible
- Cost of providing internal managerial services—benchmarked comparisons
- Perception of efficiency of key work procedures and flows
- Stretching the financial allocations
- Staff productivity (turnover, absenteesim, research outputs)

❏ Has *the organization kept its relevance over time?*
● Program revisions
● Adaptation of mission
● Meeting stakeholders needs
● Adapting to environment
● Reputation
● Sustainability over time
● Entrepreneurship

❏ Is *the organization financially viable?*
● Organization has multiple sources of fund
● Funding sources are reliable over time
● Funding is linked to growth or changes occurring

How well is the organization performing?

Chapter Two

THE ENABLING ENVIRONMENT AND ORGANIZATIONAL PERFORMANCE

Organizations do not exist in a vacuum. Each organization is set in a particular environment to which it is inextricably linked. This environment provides multiple contexts that affect the organization and its performance, what it produces, and how it operates (Nabli and Nugent, 1989). As we refine and extend the original framework for organizational assessment, the concept of an enabling environment is key to understanding and explaining the forces that help shape the character and performance of organizations (Scott, 1995).

Many development projects implemented within organizations either partially or fully fail because the intervention does not adequately address the enabling environment within which the organization operates (UNDP, 1993). For example, some development loans have channelled resources into new equipment, and then into training staff to use the new equipment. However, when this is carried out in the context of a centralized civil service that lacks the policies to keep trained people on the job, the new equipment and training may become counter-productive. Some loan projects fail because the executing agencies are operating in tumultuous environments that limit their ability to carry the project out.

Any effort to diagnose and improve the performance of an organization requires an understanding of the forces outside the organization that can facilitate or inhibit that performance (Savedoff, 1998). Enabling environments support effective and efficient organizations and individuals, and creating such environments is becoming an increasingly important aspect of development assistance (Picciotto and Weisner, 1998).

This chapter describes the enabling environment and examines it from a diagnostic perspective. It clarifies what are often hazy concepts and relationships between organizations and the environments in which they operate. The chapter also touches briefly on issues that emerge in analyzing an organization's environment, and provides guiding questions for the challenging task of examining that environment.

DEFINITIONS

Chapter One posited that the enabling environment is made up of the administrative, technological, political, economic, socio-cultural, and stakeholder factors (Lusthaus, Anderson and Murphy, 1995). This was consistent with the strategic management literature and served as a helpful categorization system. As we worked with international financial institutions that were more involved at the sectoral and institutional levels, we became more aware of the important interaction that occurs when banks intervene at the systems and organizational level. Organizations need to be able to diagnose the enabling environment, and also build competence to both influence and adapt to it as that environment evolves (Savedoff, 1998).

In this context, we built a matrix to better understand the link between our past approach and a more institutionally grounded approach to assessment that includes the components of *rules*, *ethos* and *capabilities*, each of which will be discussed in this chapter.

Rules are referred to in institutional economics literature as "institutions" (North, 1995). *Rules or institutions are the formal laws and codes that positively or negatively influence the behavior of organizations through the incentives and constraints they provide or impose.* There are rules for all dimensions of the environment: some rules are formal while others are informal and accepted by everybody. Some rules are explicit, while some are implicit. Some are codified, others less so. The codified rules tend to be found in political and administrative environments.

Institutional ethos embraces the largely informal rules of a society; that is, the history, cultural values, norms and taboos of the milieu within which organizations function. Like rules and other unwritten societal expectations, the institutional ethos imposes constraints on the behavior of organizations and the people who work within them. Although the various aspects of institutional ethos are difficult to measure and evaluate, they are nonetheless extremely important in molding the behavior and performance of organizations that evolve within a given environment.

Capabilities include labor market pools, the natural resources and geographic assets or limitations of a country or region, as well as the infrastructure and technology available. The significance

COMPONENTS OF THE ORGANIZATIONAL ENVIRONMENT

	RULES	ETHOS	CAPABILITIES
Administrative/ Legal	Legal framework	Attitudes toward enforcement	Ability to develop and enforce laws and policies
Technology	Protect intellectual property	Social attitudes to innovation	Product development, R&D capability
Political	Government type (democratic, authoritarian)	Attitudes toward civil society	Ability to organize civil society among other groups; knowledge of the electorate; degree of transparency
Economic	Clarity and usefulness of economic rules, interest rate policies, etc.	Attitudes toward civil society	Ability to develop competition policy framework and examine industrial sectors, societal databases, levels of competition, low transaction costs
Ecological	Environmental protection laws affecting organizations and individuals, role of geography	Attitudes toward the environment and its effect on organizations	Ability to assess environmental impact and to adapt
Stakeholder	Labor rights, occupational safety rules on competition	Attitudes toward not-for-profit, public and business sectors	Ability of groups to influence
Socio-cultural	Religious norms	Perception toward gender issues	Ability to shift social and cultural attitudes

MARKET REFORMS: CREATING A LEGAL FRAMEWORK TO SUPPORT PRIVATE SECTOR DEVELOPMENT[1]

Mongolia began to move away politically and culturally from Soviet domination with the onset of perestroika in 1984. In 1990, Mongolia began dismantling its centrally planned command economy and introduced a wide range of market-oriented reforms, including tax and legal reforms. Legal discrimination against private sector activities was removed in 1988, and restrictions on private ownership of herds were eliminated in 1991. These measures and others strengthened the viability of private organizations and resulted in the expansion of the private sector in Mongolia.

[1] Taken from Hahm (1993).

of these capabilities for development has long been recognized. They were often the reason for imperial or colonial relationships. We use the term "capability" to denote the internal resources at a given point in time. We also use the term capability in the environment section to distinguish it from our use of "capacity"—a term reserved in this book for discussions on organizations. In characterizing these resources, we prefer the active term "capability," which denotes power or the ability to do something (Morgan, 1998). Thus, countries want to build on their capabilities and organizations on their capacities to create an enabling environment generally targeted for them.

To the extent that an environment lacks adequate labor market pools, infrastructure and technology, the availability of these valuable resources to organizations will be limited. This is likely to affect the way they function and what they can achieve. While it is not impossible for an organization to import or develop these resources on its own, this may come with a high cost that will erode organizational efficiency (Datta and Nugent, 1998).

ETHNICITY AND HUMAN RESOURCE MANAGEMENT

In a country where ethnic tensions were strong and divisive, it was noted that in the private sector—and particularly in the financial and banking sectors—access to upward mobility in organizations and promotions were largely influenced by the ethnic origin of the employee. As a consequence, the least privileged ethnic group tended to gravitate toward public service.

> **HOW GEOGRAPHY CAN CHALLENGE ORGANIZATIONAL PERFORMANCE**
>
> The Bahamas has over 700 islands, a geographical reality that has had a tremendous impact on the country's Ministry of Education. Given its mandate to educate all children in the country, the Ministry has had to identify service delivery mechanisms that could reach children located in every part of the archipelago nation.

These three components of the enabling environment are inter-dependent in very significant ways. For example, the capability of a nation to develop its own infrastructure or to adapt and effectively use foreign technology is often affected by rules such as cultural and intellectual property rights, patents or copyrights. These are not the only factors in the external environment that affect organizations, but are among the most important identifiable factors that can help us understand and explain organizational performance.

RULES

The "rules of the game" of a society are one of the most important ingredients of the enabling environment (Datta and Nugent, 1998). They oil the economic and social machinery. All societies require appropriate rules, as well as fair and efficient mechanisms by which they can be enforced. Organizations must pursue their goals within a legal or regulatory structure that facilitates or inhibits their work. Governments and governance have significant influence on the nature of rules in society and how effectively these rules are enforced.

Administrative and Political Rules

Administrative and political rules are embedded in constitutions, traditional and common laws, charters, statutes and civil codes, some of which have significant economic implications. All organizations have special functions within a society. They exist to meet certain needs of society. For example, governments legally set up Ministries of the Environment because of a functional need to protect the environment. The government sets out the rules that define the ministry, and by so doing, outlines the relationship other organizations have with that ministry (Desormeaux, 1998).

Donors and lenders generally agree that political economy issues are important determinants of the success of programs that they support in the developing world. But while donors and lenders often require economic reforms as a condition for their support, they seldom provide the direct assistance needed to carry out and institutionalize such reforms. These organizations need to translate their concerns into action by allocating more assistance for institutional reforms (Weisner, 1998).

Political economy variables that affect the likelihood of successful development reforms are covered extensively in the political economy literature (Tommasi and Velasco, 1995; Bates and Krueger, 1993; Haggard and Kaufman, 1992). These variables include social conflicts, political instability, the type of government (dictatorship, free market, conservative, liberal, populist), whether the government is democratically elected, the tenure of the government in office, and government transparency.

In undertaking institutional reform, it is important to understand the country's constitution and laws, and to determine who has the power to change them. It is considered good policy to focus on reforming incentive structures to empower beneficiaries and to provide choices.

Economic Rules

Economic rules are embedded in contract, partnership and corporate laws, the financial order, and other regular and ad-hoc rules promulgated by bodies such as central banks to control interest rates, imports, exports and local and foreign investments (Clague et al., 1997).

Property rights profoundly affect organizations and the markets within which they operate. The rules governing property rights *give individuals, groups or organizations power to control scarce resources and to enjoy their valuable attributes* (Eggertsson, 1996). Land laws, for example, give individuals and organizations the power to control and enjoy the benefits of a piece of land (Ensminger, 1997; Nye, 1997).

Labor contracts, also based on law, *give an organization the right or power to enjoy the services of a valuable scarce resource—labor.* Contracts are a means by which organizations and individuals protect their property rights, and these contracts are grounded in law (Engerman, 1997; Nabli and Nugent, 1989). In fact, an organization can be perceived of as a set of contracts—among shareholders and owners, between shareholders and managers, between managers and workers, and between managers and other stakeholders (creditors, clients, customers, etc.). Thus, the failure or lack of enforcement of rules governing contracts and property rights can seriously affect organizational performance (Chhibber, 1998; Nugent, 1998).

Transaction costs include the costs of privately enforcing property rights, among other costs (North, 1990). When the public mechanisms that officially enforce property rights in society are inefficient or unreliable, organizations and individuals must privately institute internal controls to preserve their rights over the resources in question, raising their transaction costs. In such situations, informal rules and enforcement devices often evolve and operate outside the purview of the official or formal institutional structure (Eriksson, 1998; Greenhill, 1995).

Economic rules and their enforcement actually play a significant role in determining the structure of organizations in an economy, as seen in the accompanying box about Brazil.

Enforcement of Rules

The enforcement of rules or institutions is at least as important as the rules themselves (Kaji, 1998). Nowhere is this more apparent than in the financial sector, where
banks must be reasonably sure that loan contracts can and will be enforced in the
event that clients default (Nugent, 1998). As is evident in many developing countries, unsound rules and enforcement systems in the financial sector can have negative ripple effects on the willingness of lending organizations to lend, on the borrowing organization's ability to borrow and invest, and hence on the performance of
the entire economy. Problems of rural credit in many developing countries under-
score the importance of the enforceability of rules, as seen in the accompanying box.

TRADITIONAL LOAN ENFORCEMENT AND RURAL CREDIT

Formal credit institutions using traditional banking methods were not very successful in
providing rural credit in developing countries. Part of the problem was the uncertainty of enforcing loan contracts with people who are inherently poor and who are
engaged in the risky business of agriculture—where yields are highly influenced by
the vagaries of nature. Enforcement of traditional loan contracts is linked to the bor-
rower's ability to provide collateral, which most peasants lack.

Necessary Attributes of Rules

Enforcement of formal rules is largely based on legally sanctioned coercion or force,
or the threat of it (Chong and Claderon, 1997). The effectiveness of enforcement,
however, depends to some extent on whether people see the rules as being worthy
of respect. If rules are not seen as fair or fairly enforced, individuals and organizations have greater incentive to evade them, increasing the difficulty and cost of
enforcement. Therefore, among other attributes, good rules should be credible, fairly and evenly enforced, predictable and flexible (Burki and Perry, 1998).

Credibility refers to the extent to which rules and their enforcement systems
command respect from those affected by them. The credibility of rules or institutions depends partly on low transaction costs and fairness. In this context, low transaction costs refer to the capacity of rules and enforcement of them to facilitate and
accelerate economic exchanges and interactions using minimal resources. Fairness

is the degree to which rules and their enforcement are applied consistently and impartially from one person or group to another (Hunter and Lewis, 1997).

Predictability is the extent to which actors within the environment have to cope with unexpected changes in rules and policies. Flexibility is the extent to which rules and their enforcement mechanisms change over time in response to the needs of society. An important consideration in guaranteeing ownership of the rules is to ensure those affected by them actively participate in creating them, either directly or indirectly (Lal, 1996). This point is best illustrated in the accompanying box by contrasting two irrigation systems in Nepal in the early 1990s.

IRRIGATION SYSTEMS IN NEPAL

In 1993-94, data from the Nepal Irrigation Institutions and Systems (NIIS) showed that farmer-governed systems performed far better than agency-managed systems. The agency-managed system was a government system created as a funded intervention to improve irrigation results. Actors in these systems were not involved in making the rules that governed them. Most of the professional staff was employed under the terms of the bureaucratic civil service system, where remuneration was fixed and promotion was largely based on seniority, rather than performance. On the other hand, actors in the farmer-managed systems set their own rules and operated their own system whereby they evolved their own social capital, i.e., their set of shared knowledge, understandings, institutions or rules, and patterns of interaction. Therefore, they had more incentive to perform (Ostrom, 1997).

Assessing Rules

An important empirical question of interest to development practitioners and agencies is how to analyze a given institutional framework and its rule enforcement mechanisms (Clague et al., 1997). Clearly, development agencies and international financial institutions have devised a wide assortment of methodologies to assess the national and sectoral rules within which organizations operate. It is the direct effect of rules on the organization that affects organizational life.

Thus, organizational assessments by development agencies and international financial institutions should examine the quality of rules. This should be done when evaluating the performance of projects these institutions already support, when analyzing the capacities of a potential executing agency for a loan, and even when searching for promising organizational candidates with whom to work. Indeed, the key to successful development lending is to identify effective organizational partners to support. Good candidates for such partnerships are organizations that genuinely seek reform, and that already either have a conducive institutional environment or are honestly committed to creating one (Chhibber, 1998).

In this regard, international agencies must be prepared to devote part of their assistance to institutional diagnosis and reform, without which many of the other development efforts they support are doomed to produce less than satisfactory results. Indeed, some international agencies—particularly the World Bank—have focused their development efforts toward interventions at the institutional level, moving away from several decades of support at the individual and organizational levels.

The importance of using objective quantitative measures to evaluate or assess rules and their enforcement systems is well recognized by development practitioners. But the difficulty in obtaining such measures is also noted (Burki and Perry, 1998), although less rigorous, subjective quantitative measures compiled by credit risk agencies do exist for many countries. These measures are computed on various scales, and they include indices of corruption, red tape, efficiency of legal systems, and political stability. Although there is increasing interest in the rules of the game, and a number of instruments have been developed to assess them, many of these are too detailed and require modification if they are to be used for assessing the environment within which organizations operate (Manning, 2000).

At a more pragmatic level, assessing the rules means identifying the extent to which the existing rules are helping or inhibiting organizations, or facilitating the loan or project execution. Assessment always must examine the degree to which the risk level for the loan or the project is associated with enforcement of the rules.

One aspect of an organizational assessment is to characterize the rules and enforcement mechanisms in the organization's environment. The questions in the accompanying box should be included in assessment of an organization's environment.

INSTITUTIONAL ETHOS

As societies evolve over time, they gather unique historical experiences and acquire a set of cultural values, norms, religious precepts and taboos. These implicit or unwritten codes of conduct can be grouped together with the history of the society under the broad heading *institutional ethos*. In the literature on institutions, this is also referred to as the "informal rules of the game." It is these informal rules that often give insights into why some rules are enforced and others are not; or why some people have power, when their organizational position indicates that they should not. The informal rules of society help seemingly irrational behavior appear rational.

History

The history of a society is the totality of its experiences—successes, failures, wars, disasters, and the emergence of great leaders and their influence on the society. Indeed, history matters. These events and experiences influence the attitudes, beliefs, determination and moral principles of individuals and organizations within the society or environment.

Thus, history helps to shape the cultural values, religious beliefs, ethics and taboos that directly affect what individuals and organizations do or can do in a society, and how they do it. Examples of how this happens abound, ranging from America's liberalism and economic prowess, to the influence of Japanese culture on that nation's industrial success, to economic stagnation in some developing countries that has been attributed to factors such as inhibiting traditional cultures or even colonialism (Silos, 1991).

Enforcement of Institutional Ethos

Unlike formal rules, which generally derive their legitimacy from the law, the components of institutional ethos gain legitimacy from the fact they are morally governed and culturally supported (Engerman, 1997). The enforcement of formal rules tends to be based on legal sanctions, whereas cultural values and mores are generally enforced through the prescriptive and evaluative processes inherent in social life (Skinner, 1996).

Sometimes cultural considerations are more important than formal legal considerations in creating an effective framework for enforcement mechanisms for rules. As development agencies target and evaluate the performance of their partners and executing agencies in developing countries, it is essential that they identify the aspects of institutional ethos that facilitate or constrain the work of the organizations they support.

As seen in the accompanying box, the case of the Grameen Bank illustrates how socio-cultural factors have been crucial to creating a successful rural banking system in Bangladesh (Khandker, Khalily and Khan, 1995).

ENFORCEMENT AND SOCIAL COLLATERAL: SUCCESS OF GRAMEEN BANKS

While many traditional rural credit banks have failed, the Grameen Bank has succeeded in effectively delivering rural credit. This is largely because its banking method is based on social collateral and socio-cultural links among borrowers, rather than on the traditional physical collateral required by other banks. Fear of being ostracized from society (or from some social group), and pressure from group members, can be quite effective in ensuring that clients honor their credit contracts.

Culture

Cultural norms and mores include a society's habits, ways of thinking, values, and informal unwritten standards. These socio-cultural forces operate at local, national and regional levels, and have a profound influence on the way organizations conduct their business and what they value in terms of outputs and effects (Mauro, 1995). For example, the mores of an indigenous culture have a bearing on the work ethic and on the way in which people relate to one another in that culture. Cultural traits affect society's degree of risk tolerance (or risk avoidance), as well as support for individual initiative, and such traits in turn can have negative or positive influences on organizations (Engerman, 1997).

Questions: Institutional Ethos

- What are the memorable events in the society's history as they relate to the organization (history of research, banking, etc.)?
- What is noteworthy in the evolution of the industry or sector to which the organization pertains?
- Are there inducements and incentives or disincentives for a particular type of organization, its product, or its methods of doing things (incentives/disincentives that are culturally based or historically influenced)?
- What historical, cultural or religious factors in the society are likely to negatively affect the organization (ethnic or other class struggles, religious intolerance and fanaticism, violence and criminality, corruption and nepotism, etc.)?
- What historical, cultural or religious factors in the society are likely to positively affect the organization?

CAPABILITIES

In addition to rules and ethos, every society has a certain combination of resources that influences the type and scale of activities undertaken by individuals and organizations, as well as how successful their efforts are likely to be. These include natural resources, human resources, financial resources, infrastructure (transport, roads, electricity, telecommunications), and technology. Together they form what we call "capabilities." They combine with rules and institutional ethos to create an enabling or inhibiting environment for organizations and development.

Of importance to all countries is the worldwide concern about the environment. Modern societies view protection of the environment as an essential objective. In developing countries, explicit environmental approval is frequently required before an organization develops a new project. Failure by the organization to comply with any of the regulations pertaining to the environment may result in political pressures from domestic or foreign environmental activists.

Dimensions

Perceptions about which of these capabilities or resources is more critical for development has shifted over time from natural resources to human resources, capital and technology. The emerging consensus is that an enabling environment is a combination of all the resources and the institutional framework (rules and ethos). There is no single ideal combination. Experience shows that in a highly interdependent world, it is possible to make up for the shortage of one resource (e.g., natural resources in Japan) by creating linkages and strengthening or developing other resources (e.g., human capital and technology).

Thus, from a macro perspective for development assistance, the question is no longer whether more training or more transfer of equipment and technology is most crucial for development in developing countries. Rather, the question is, what combination of training, technology, institutional reform and so forth is appropriate for creating an enabling macro-environment that maximizes resource utilization within a specific context?

Resources

These issues are discussed in the growing literature on capacity building and development, and it is not our objective to review them here. It is important to understand, however, that the availability or shortage of these capabilities at the macro level can influence the performance of specific organizations at the micro level. Organizations need good human resources and other core resources (infrastructure, technology and finance) to improve their capacity to perform (see Chapter Three). However, they must rely to a great extent on the macro environment to provide these resources. The amount and quality of available resources will depend on the institutional and policy environment.

Labor Force

The quantity and quality of the basic labor force available to both public and private sector organizations is influenced to some extent by the quality of the country's formal and technical education. This, in turn, is a function of the policies and rules the government puts in place over time to create the necessary incentives to develop an effective system of education. In other words, a sustained long-term solution to solving human resource capacity gaps in developing countries requires much more than providing scholarships to a handful of citizens to study in universities in developed countries. A more radical approach is needed, requiring institutional reforms to create the right incentives.

Access to Technology and Systems

The same argument applies to the development of indigenous technology and efficient financial systems. This point illustrates the overriding influence of rules and, as noted earlier, the interdependence of the various components of an enabling environment. Before launching ambitious programs to develop capabilities, it is important to conduct a thorough institutional analysis. This involves mapping the institutional environment in terms of politics, administrative capacity, culture, etc. in a manner that includes all stakeholders and measures their level of ownership and commitment to reform.

Questions: Capabilities

- To what extent does the organization have access to an adequate labor market? How important are labor constraints to organizational performance?
- To what extent does the organization have access to an adequate capital market? How important are capital market constraints to organizational performance?
- To what extent does the organization have access to appropriate technology so that it can effectively and efficiently provide its goods and services?
- Is the local infrastructure (road and transport systems, electricity and telecommunications) adequate to permit private and public sector organizations to carry out their business effectively and efficiently?
- Are technology policies and investment inducements supportive of the organization under review?
- Are there effective national policies on science and technology (including information technology)? If so, how well are these policies implemented?
- Is the system of government and the institutional milieu conducive for the acquisition of technology by organizations and the development of local technology?

CONCLUSIONS

To summarize, there are various factors outside the organization that profoundly influence its structure, performance and, in some cases, its very existence. These factors combine to create an enabling environment within which individuals and organizations achieve their goals in a more or less efficient manner. To facilitate discussion within the context of our evolving institutional and organizational framework, we identified three forces in the enabling environment: the formal rules of the game, the institutional ethos, and capabilities

The discussion of the enabling environment focused primarily on the distal environment, which relates to rules that are not specific to any one organization or set of organizations, but bear on the activities and performance of all organizations. From the point of view of a particular organization, however, it is useful to distinguish the proximal environment from the distal environment. This proximal environment comprises rules that are designed to regulate a specific organization or the sector to which it belongs (private sector, public sector, NGO, manufacturing sector, service sector, etc.).

In conclusion, the concepts in this chapter suggest a number of questions that are of crucial importance to donors and development agencies, and to the success of their existing and future interventions in developing countries:

- To what extent, and in what ways, can external investment agencies change the enabling environment?
- Under what conditions would those agencies want to support an organization, or a set of organizations, without investing in creating an enabling environment?
- How receptive to change is the target group or groups likely to be?
- How receptive are the politicians and other beneficiaries of the existing system likely to be?
- To what extent would resistance to change from various groups deter the required change?

A fuller list of questions concerning all of the issues regarding an enabling environment may be found in Appendix 1.

Chapter Three

CAPACITY

For some time now, a number of development agencies have stressed that investment choices should focus on building the capacity of local organizations to solve their development problems. The United Nations Development Programme (1999) identifies capacity development as "a key strategy for its work". The International Development Research Centre (1987) describes efforts to ensure sustainable organizational development through a focused and holistic effort to build the capacity of its funded partners. Other international agencies such as the Inter-American Development Bank, the World Bank and UNICEF have a stake in and are committed to ensuring that the organizations they support in developing countries build the capacity necessary to stand on their own feet to meet their repayment commitments.

The experience of these development agencies indicates that facilitating change at the organizational level is conceptually and practically more difficult and complex an undertaking than simple project support. At the center of this complexity is our embryonic understanding of building organizational capacity in developing contexts (Lusthaus, Adrien and Perstinger, 1999).

Our framework for viewing organizational capacity entails eight interrelated areas that underlie an organization's performance. These are *strategic leadership, organizational structure, human resources, financial management, infrastructure, program and services management, process management, and inter-organizational linkages*. Each of those areas addressed in this chapter involves various sub-components that range in importance from organization to organization (see chart).

STRATEGIC LEADERSHIP

Strategic leadership refers to all those activities that set the course for the organization and help it stay on course in service of its mission. Strategic leadership is associated with the organization's vision, as well as with the ideas and actions that make the organization unique. It is the process of setting clear organizational goals and directing the efforts of staff and other stakeholders toward fulfilling organizational objectives (Mintzberg and Quinn, 1995).

In essence, therefore, strategic leadership has to do with the organization's ability to influence its internal and external stakeholders so that they will support organizational directions. Strategic leadership needs to empower its members to create the changes that are necessary for an organization to perform and survive (Byrd, 1987). It goes beyond simple planning, in that it creates ways of clarifying and obtaining organizational goals by looking within and outside the organization. It sets the stage for organizational action and the methodologies the organization will use to produce the results required Thus, an organization's strategic leadership involves developing ways of inspiring organizational members and stakeholders to perform in ways that attain the mission, while adapting to or buffering external forces.

Definition and Dimensions

Leadership is a key ingredient in this component. Some management scientists believe that many organizations are relatively under-led and over-managed (Kotter, 1990). Our experience shows this is true of many organizations where leaders or senior managers often focus too much attention on adaptations to the internal environment and structures, and too little on the wider, changing external environment (Hesselbein, Goldsmith and Beckhard, 1996).

This much-needed holistic external focus helps leaders identify and define the organization's long-term future position, as well as design and execute strategies that will successfully take the organization there. Many organizations lack strategic leadership, defined here as *the ability to manage through others, to foresee opportunities and constraints, to help the organization change successfully and accordingly in the process of effecting change, and to accommodate and reconcile both external and internal conditions.*

Accommodating and reconciling external and internal conditions is a complex task. The outcome of effective strategic leadership is aligned direction and action. A strategically led organization will be continuously engaged in the process of changing, adapting and following a path that makes sense to its members and to the external stakeholders who fund the organization or confer reputation.

THE IDB AND STRATEGIC LEADERSHIP

Many organizations today are carefully looking at their mandate and the way they are going about engaging in it. This is true of small environmental NGOs, as well as large international agencies. For the past several years, the Inter-American Development Bank has strategically refocused its work and its approach to that work. Discussions at all levels within the organization have led to new ways of working and thinking. In a working paper prepared by the institution, senior officials at the operational level analyze the strengths and weaknesses of their internal and external environment. It is part vision, part plan, part reinventing who they are—in other words, it is an attempt at strategic leadership, that is, to affect change by analyzing internal and external conditions.

Strategic leadership consists of three main dimensions: leadership, strategic planning and niche management

Leadership

Leadership is basically the process through which leaders influence the attitudes, behaviors and values of others towards organizational goals (Vecchio, 1995). Indeed, no one can deny its critical importance to the success of any organization, no matter where the organization is located or what it does. Salopek (1998) outlines four fundamental qualities of leadership, each of which has several specialized and associated competencies. These qualities relate to the ability to become and act as the following:

- Collaborators skilled at facilitating, coaching and fostering dialogue;
- Innovators skilled at visioning, championing and diffusing;
- Integrators skilled at organizing, improving and bridging;
- Producers skilled at targeting, improving and measuring.

An effective leader must possess these qualities and competencies, and must merge them into a single leadership quality that personifies what, taken together, they stand for (Bennis and Goldsmith, 1997). This style becomes operationalized in the leader's organizational actions.

The need for leadership qualities is not restricted to executive senior managers, but extends to workers at all levels of the organization. Leadership exists at many places inside the organization, both formally and informally. Formal leadership, exercised by those appointed or elected to positions of authority, entails activities such as setting direction, providing symbols of the mission, ensuring that tasks are done, supporting resource development, and modeling the importance of clients.

On the other hand, persons who become influential exert informal leadership because they possess special skills or resources valued or needed by others (Handy, 1997). Examples of informal leadership include spearheading the reorganization of the professional library, or initiating an innovative, multi-disciplinary approach to a research problem (Tichy, 1997).

In organizations with effective leadership, each worker believes that he or she should and can contribute to the success of the organization, act as a partner, be largely self-directed, and assume responsibility for his or her actions and contributions. As a group, workers feel empowered and have the requisite knowledge, skills, opportunity, guidelines and personal initiative to perform effectively (Nanus, 1989).

Questions: Leadership

- *Do people in the organization support formal leadership?*
- *Do people in the organization take on positive informal leadership roles?*
- *Does the organization recognize the importance of distributive leadership?*
- *Is staff throughout the organization willing to take on leadership roles?*
- *Is staff willing to try new suggestions made by those in leadership positions?*
- *Are both internal and external stakeholders supportive of the formal organizational leadership?*
- *Does all staff have an opportunity to suggest changes in the organization?*
- *Is leadership that supports organizational goals rewarded?*

Strategic Planning

Strategic planning refers to the pattern of calculated responses to the environment, including resource deployment, that enable an organization to achieve its goals. It is a disciplined and creative process for determining where the organization should be in the future and how to take it there (Graf, Hemmasi and Strong, 1996). Strategic planning entails formulating and implementing activities that lead to long-term organizational success. It is essentially a decision-making process that involves a search for answers to simple but critical and fundamental questions: What is the organization doing? How is it doing what it does? Where should it be going in the future? What should it be doing now to get there?

Strategic planning encompasses issues spanning the entire spectrum of the organization, from introspective questions of what the organization's personality is or ought to be, to strategic operational issues connecting the focus on the future with work to do to move the organization forward. The strategic plan itself is a written document, setting out the specific goals, priorities and tactics the organization intends to employ to ensure good performance (Kaplan and Norton, 1996).

Strategic planning is a participatory process engendering a shared commitment to organizational directions (Ketchen, Thomas and McDaniel, 1996). Formulating strategy begins with identifying or clarifying goals and objectives and determining the methods for reaching them. It involves exploring such fundamental questions as the following: What major services does the organization offer? Who are its clients and what type and quality of services would they prefer? Do workers agree with organizational direction? In what new directions should the organization move?

Thus, strategic planning must typically include a scan of opportunities, threats and constraints presented by the environment. This means that the organization must repeatedly ask itself what potential or pending actions are likely to influence (positively or negatively) what it does and plans to do? How can the organization forestall or mitigate the negative influences, as well as take advantage of the potential opportunities?

Another strategic issue for the survival of an organization is the acquisition of resources in the vital areas of funding, technology, infrastructure and personnel. Strategic planning must adequately pursue these resources by anticipating and capitalizing on opportunities in the external environment that might yield or support them. It also means predicting threats to organizational resources and intervening (politically, in general) to ensure that organizational performance and survival are safeguarded (Korey, 1995).

This level of leadership and intervention generally transpires between the senior executive of the organization and the governing body in the country. Resource acquisition entails constantly being on the lookout to create opportunities that will augment the organization's resources. This is accomplished by forming new alliances and partnerships, and by forging new ways of thinking about generating resources (Baron, 1995).

For strategies to become operational, they need to be communicated, processed and revised according to feedback from stakeholders, both internal and external. All members of the organization need to work toward making the strategic plan a reality, from senior management down to the most junior worker (Mintzberg

---

OTHER FACTORS NEED CAREFUL EXAMINATION

Of critical importance in strategic planning and strategy formulation is the need to take into account broader institutional and socio-political factors. Each element of strategy (objectives, activities and resources) is constrained by political, social, technological and economic environmental variables, particularly in public organizations. For instance, in the case of certain research organizations, the science and technology policy of the government is a vitally important variable. In the same way, changes in macroeconomic policies that affect interest rates and investment rules in developing countries are crucial to both local organizations and their funding partners.

and Quinn, 1995). Implementing strategy requires matching resources and activities to objectives and, if required, scaling activities to fit resource constraints (human, financial, technological and infrastructural).

Questions: Strategic Planning

- Is there a formal or informal organizational strategy? Is the strategy supporting a high level of performance?
- Do the board of governors, senior managers and staff members support the organization's strategy?
- Is the strategy generally accepted and supported in the organization?
- Has the strategy helped clarify priorities and set indicators, thus giving the organization a way to assess its performance?
- Is the strategy used as a way to help make decisions?
- Is the strategy an impediment or a facilitator to capacity building or improved performance?
- Is there a process for clarifying and revising the organization's strategy?
- Is there an ongoing process for scanning the environment to consider potential threats and opportunities?
- Does the organizational strategy identify the opportunities and constraints regarding core resource areas related to improving or detracting from performance?

Niche Management

In today's global and highly competitive society, the success of an organization is, in part, predicated on its ability to establish a unique role within the society by offering a unique service or product. *Niche management essentially involves identifying and then concentrating on a competitively valuable capability (or set of capabilities) that the organization possesses more of, or can do better, than its rivals.*

Niche management involves identifying the distinctive competence the organization possesses, with the primary objective of gaining a competitive edge in the marketplace. Niche management entails carving out a particular area for the organization in the marketplace that matches its particular expertise and distinctive competencies. A niche within an organization is a platform for interaction. It emerges out of a process of interaction shaped by many actors, both internally and externally (Beaton, 1994).

In the private sector, the marketing function evaluates an organization's image or position in the marketplace and reaches strategic decisions concerning target markets, services and products (Beesley, 1995). This model is not so far afield from public sector organizations, which, for their survival, must increasingly cultivate appropriate clients and other stakeholders, ensure that their products and services meet the needs of the consuming public, and fund providers (Cohen, 1993). However, though public sector organizations are gradually becoming interested in their own niche, they are slower to react to the importance of being identified in a niche and tend to react more slowly to changes in clients and beneficiaries.

In increasing numbers of public sector organizations, as well as in some non-governmental organizations, niche management may be limited to developing capabilities to deliver a product or service in such a distinctive way as to guarantee continued future funding from government and other agencies (often in preference over rival organizations). Building relationships and keeping abreast of the vicissitudes of

---

FINDING THE APPROPRIATE NICHE FOR THE CANADA MORTGAGE AND HOUSING CORPORATION

Canada established a number of independent agencies that initially were part of the government structure, but are now separate legal entities that are either independent, or partially or totally owned by the government. One organization that has been reviewed as part of Canada's re-engineering exercise to improve the effectiveness and efficiency of the government is the Canada Mortgage and Housing Corporation (CMHC).

The CMHC has been Canada's national housing agency for over 50 years. Amendments to the National Housing Act in June 1999 gave CMHC a specific mandate to promote and support the export of Canadian housing products, services and expertise around the world. The Canadian Housing Export Centre (CHEC) was established in 1997 to help the housing industry market its excellence abroad and to coordinate the export of CMHC's own knowledge.

Domestically, the CMHC was successful in promoting home ownership and supporting the Canadian home development industry. However, the development of that industry is also linked to its ability to be internationally competitive. Thus, as part of its operational activity and, ultimately, its performance as an agency, CMHC needs to develop ways to support internationalization of this industry. But what is appropriate for CMHC to support? Where are the points of comparative advantage? Clearly, not all aspects of an industry developed to meet a "northern" housing market are relevant around the world.

---

the external environment are integral parts of this management process. It means that external communications are important, as these may be needed to stimulate funding, or to stimulate awareness.

Niche management is an organizational function that forces managers to look beyond internal matters to consider the wider environment and the broader issues of the time. If this function is neglected, the organization's ability to adapt to the changing global situation is severely eroded.

Identifying distinctive competencies and client needs is particularly challenging in developing countries because of the chronic lack of information. It makes it difficult to gather information on competitors and on current as well as potential clients. Certain aspects of niche management are more difficult in these countries. However, as organizations in developing countries mature, information will improve, and infor-

---

REINVENTING THEMSELVES: THE BANGLADESH RELIEF COMMITTEE AND THE INTERNATIONAL CENTER FOR DIARRHEAL DISEASE RESEARCH

Two important not-for-profit organizations in Bangladesh are the International Center for Diarrheal Disease Research (ICDDR) and the Bangladesh Relief Committee (BRAC). Both illustrate the importance of information as a basis for an organization to evolve.

BRAC is one of the most successful development NGOs in the developing world. It has revenues of over $257 million and works with millions of poor people in Bangladesh in a wide assortment of development areas. However, times are changing in the developing world. First, on a global basis, development assistance has declined. This will diminish the ability of BRAC to access development assistance as a major aspect of its own growth and development. Second, it is increasingly clear that new approaches to development need to be invented if poverty is to be reduced. Armed with market-oriented information, BRAC is thus creating new niches for itself and the development NGO community.

One such venture is its entry into the world of information technology training. This developed as a joint venture with IBM to create a major training center for potential information technology professionals in Bangladesh. The Private Sector-NGO alliance is a major partnership to support the development of the country's information technology sector. It is a government priority, but one that it is difficult for the government to implement.

In a different context, but with a similar analytical use of information, ICDDR in Bangladesh is trying to transform itself into a "Center of Excellence" with a focus on nutrition as opposed to diarrheal diseases. ICDDR research indicates that significant progress can be made to combat diarrheal diseases if ICDDR works on the nutritional side of the problem. This opens up new avenues of research and work for this world-class research center.

mation focusing on targeted issues (niches) will be better integrated into the decision-making process (Beaton, 1994).

Questions: Niche Management

- Has the organization defined its unique place (or places) within a sector in terms of philosophy, mission and goals?
- Are its strengths matched with the niche selected?
- Does the organization do competitive strength assessments to identify core and distinctive competencies that reveal its strengths and weaknesses within its niche (competitive position)?
- Does the organization seek information about the products and services that clients want?
- Does the organization collect information on its sector (market) and its role inside the sector or market?
- Do potential clients or customers know, or can they find out about, programs and services that represent the niche?
- Is equity served through this niche? For example, are women and other under-represented groups served within the niche?
- Does the organization have sufficient financial support to keep its niche? Does it communicate or promote its niche to both internal and external stakeholders?

ORGANIZATIONAL STRUCTURE

The ability of an organization to structure and restructure itself to adapt to changing internal and external conditions is important for maximizing organizational performance. Unlike other capacities, the structuring and restructuring of an organization does not formally occur on a constant basis; however, adaptations of structure are always occurring. Organizational structure is defined as the ability of an organization to divide labor and assign roles and responsibilities to individuals and groups in the organization, as well as the process by which the organization attempts to coordinate its labor and groups. It is also concerned with the relative relationships between the divisions of labor:

- Who has authority over whom?
- How and why should an organization divide labor individually and by grouping people?

- How should organizations coordinate their work to maximize the benefits of the divisions of labor?
- What do people look for to indicate that problems are structural in nature rather than some other type of problem, such as one of leadership?

For a long time, organizational structure interested both practitioners and thinkers in the field of management. At the start of the 20th century, writings focused on formal structure (Weber, 1947), which evolved into various ways of organizing work (Taylor, 1947), which led to a period of looking at informal structure (Roethlisberger and Dickson, 1939). This evolution has, in turn, led to the variety of new approaches: adhocracy (Bennis, 1969), matrix (Galbraith, 1973), contingency (Lawrence and Lorsch, 1967), and TQM (Deming, 1986).

Debates continue over the importance of issues such as the stages of organizational development (should new organizations be structured differently than older ones?); organizational size (when should size determine how labor should be divided?); and centralization versus decentralization in terms of organizational structure. In recent years, the debate over structure has become more complicated. The field has been further enlivened by discussions about the influence of technology on structure; the importance of the governance structure; and new issues raised by feminist researchers about the very nature of organizing as well as the fundamental issues of power.

In our own work with donors (IDRC, CIDA) and development banks (IDB, World Bank), restructuring was found to be one of the frequent responses to counteract poor performance. Why is that so? Does experience indicate that restructuring provides a high probability of improving performance? What else might the restructuring do?

It is useful to think about two separate but connected aspects of organizational structure. The first is the governing structure that represents the ownership or legal guidance system of the organization. Here the structure relates to the ultimate legal and social responsibility of the organization. The second is the operating structure—how an organization transforms resources into goods and services for targeted purposes. When assessing structure, both of these aspects must be explored.

Governing Structure

In one sense, the term *governance* is used to refer to the issues and problems involved in aligning the interests of those who manage an organization with the interests of those who are responsible for organizational results, the organization's owners, and "outsiders" who have a stake in the organization. The separation of governing or ownership responsibility from management raises questions that are of strategic importance to the success or performance of any modern organization (Mueller, 1995).

In government organizations, the people of the country are the ultimate stakeholders of the governing structure. Governance is exercised through government and through a minister responsible for the specific entity (Mintzberg and Quinn, 1995). At the government level, ministers and their team manage the bureaucracy and try to link public policy and bureaucratic action.

In nongovernmental organizations, the governing structure provides an overseeing function and is responsible to act for members or in the public interest. In a private sector organization, the critical question is: What can be done to ensure that management acts in the best interests of owners or shareholders (maximize owners' wealth, which is the same thing as maximizing the value of the organization)? In other words, how should governance of the organization be structured, and what safeguards can be put in place to create congruence between governance and the personal goals of managers?

In public sector organizations, especially state enterprises, where the idea of ownership is not as clearly defined as in the private sector, the problem of governance is becoming increasingly important (CCAF, 1996). Public sector managers are frequently subjected to less rigid controls and are likely to have greater incentives to satisfy their own interests at the expense of organizational goals. Add to this the ineffective and lax institutional framework and enforcement mechanisms that characterize many intervention milieus in developing countries, and you have the perfect recipe for mass public sector mismanagement (CCAF, 1996).

Within this context of a governing structure, the board of directors and the charter of incorporation provide the legal and policy framework and direction for organizational functioning. In a wider sense, governance is conceived of as the point at which the external and internal environments meet. The governing structure addresses the problems of linking or harmonizing the conflicting interests of all stakeholders (both internal and external, including the general public) with the organization's goals and mission (Carver, 1996).

A good board of directors has its finger on the pulse of both environments. It assesses whether organizational goals are supportable and meet national development goals, as well as whether the organization is responding appropriately to major trends in the field and within the broader environment, and whether it meets the needs of those it serves.

ORGANIZATIONAL STRUCTURE: AN ONGOING PROCEDURE

In many developing countries, land ownership is a source of both wealth and power. In Belize, park land (almost one-third of all land) is officially owned by the government and managed by a government agency and an oversight board.

The critical responsibility of the government agency was to provide effective environmental management of key variables that affect national economic development. Any operational weakness or reduced impact of assigned fiscal resources would affect the sustainability of land use, forest and water resources, mining, and ultimately, the coral reefs. The management of these resources required avoiding confusion and wasteful duplication. This was important under the restrictive fiscal policy of the government and recent retrenchment exercises.

In January 1999, the agency informed the Inter-American Development Bank of its upcoming reorganizational activity. The main focus of the exercise was to develop the appropriate organizational structure, design new procedures, and train existing staff. There was a need to review the agency's strategic planning management, organizational capacity and performance, as well as to clarify organizational issues in order to improve performance and achieve results with the key stakeholders in the private and public sectors of the country.

To achieve its objectives, the agency had to coordinate the environmental activities of all its departments. The three departments and a unit, along with several interdepartmental authorities and the Office of Geology and Petroleum Committees, were created at different times in response to specific issues, and through different legislative acts. While each department and authority shared responsibility for the sustainable allocation and management of related natural resources, those linkages were not reflected in the agency's organizational and administrative procedures.

The main activities that needed to be coordinated included (a) assignment of staff, (b) budgeting of fiscal resources, (c) field coordination and matching of duties, (d) monitoring of effective use of resources, (e) impact evaluation of resource use, and (f) data management and sharing of information systems for monitoring resource use. Finally, better performance by the agency required the support of a high-level interministerial coordination mechanism to achieve effective environmental management.

The responsibility for different activities was dispersed among various government institutions. Establishment of effective arrangements for efficient interagency coordination was required. The agency is presently engaged in a medium-term restructuring process.

It is at the governance level that conflicts of interest are resolved, policy issues discussed and resolved in a timely manner, organizational policies set, and capital and operating budgets approved. The power and politics of the organization inevitably reside here, for the governing body is often a forum for airing internal demands and resolving them within funding realities. The governing body is involved with strategic direction and priorities, stakeholder representation, equity, external environmental forces (both positive and negative), and core resources.

Questions: Governing Structure

- Does the governing structure have a clearly defined way to review and set organizational direction?
- Does the governing body have a group responsible to scan the external and internal environment to understand the forces affecting the organization and its performance?
- Does the governing structure have a group that reviews safeguards and incentives to ensure that managers throughout the organization do not compromise organizational goals in the interest of their personal goals?
- Does the governing body have a group responsible to respond appropriately to major environmental trends and influences, be they social, political or economic? For instance, are both quality and equity issues reflected in the minutes and discussions?
- Does the organizational charter provide an adequate framework for creating structural means to carry out the mission of the organization? Is it adequate for dealing with the external forces challenging the organization?
- Does the governing structure have the various committees necessary to ensure legal and organizational accountability?
- Does the governing structure have the mechanisms to review and assess organizational performance and, if appropriate, create conditions to support change?

Operating Structure

The operating structure of an organization is the system of working relationships arrived at to divide and coordinate the tasks of people and groups working toward a common purpose. Most people visualize an organization's structure in terms of the familiar organizational chart. However, structure is far more than just that. It involves the division of labor, including roles, responsibility and authority, as well as the coordination of labor into units and inter- and intra-unit groupings. One must assess structure to see if it is facilitating or hindering movement toward the mission and goals (Meyer, 1995).

The task of creating appropriate and manageable work units or departments has challenged managers and students of organizational development for decades. We now realize that the "ideal" structure is the one that best fits the situation. At issue is whether or not the organizational structure supports or inhibits the capacity of the organization to perform its work.

In looking at structure, we are interested in the extent to which individuals, departments or other groupings understand their roles in the organization; whether they have the authority to carry out their roles; and whether they are accountable for their work.

Structure also includes coordination issues (Mintzberg and Quinn, 1995). Coordination is the process of linking specialized activities of individuals or groups

Questions: Operating Structure

- Are the organization's mission and goals supported by its structure?
- Are roles within the organization (groupings as well as individual) clearly defined, yet flexible enough to adapt to changing needs?
- Are departmental lines or divisions between groups coordinated to improve performance? Or are departmental lines jealously guarded, serving as impediments to collaboration?
- Does the structure support or inhibit an efficient production of goods or provision of services?
- Are coordinating units formed to facilitate performance?
- Are there clear lines of authority and accountability (individual, group and organizational)?
- Do people have the authority to set agendas that support improved performance?
- Are the work groups and units adequate for implementing the organizational strategy and improving performance?
- How centralized (versus decentralized) is decision-making? Does the existing approach have negative consequences such as impeded productivity, low morale, etc.?
- Is it clear who bears responsibility for performance? Does the structure of responsibility and authority make organizational sense and facilitate the work?
- Are the functional units adequately centralized or decentralized?
- Are work processes clear and adequately structured?
- Are quality principles embedded in the roles and responsibilities?

so they can and will work toward common ends. The coordination process helps people to work in harmony by providing systems and mechanisms for understanding and communicating about their activities.

In organizations where innovation and productivity are key, interdisciplinary teamwork is a competitive advantage. Entire networks are formed where the best minds collectively tackle difficult research problems, with each contributor bringing his or her special perspective and expertise. The ease with which the research institution facilitates interdisciplinary approaches to research projects is an indicator of organizational health.

Many variables influence organizational structure, including history, size, technology, organizational goals, strategy, governance, funding and other pressures from the external environment, the specific fields of research, and technology.

Another important structural consideration is the manner in which authority is shared. Organizations range from the decentralized to the centralized, from the highly participatory to the dictatorial. Each aspect of the structure (centralization-participatory) is a reaction to both internal and external conditions. Today, many organizations—particularly government organizations—are interested in ways to decentralize authority and increase the participation of organizational members.

In general, this interest emerges from several insights. First, organizational performance can be improved if operational decision-making is closer to the actual sources of information. Second, people working in organizations are more likely to take responsibility for their actions if they participate in the decision-making process. Whether the structure itself is centralized, decentralized or participatory, it is clear that these aspects of structure are important to improving organizational performance.

DECENTRALIZATION IN BURKINA FASO

One of the important aspects of decentralization is the devolution between national and regional bodies and municipalities. In many parts of the world, it is increasingly recognized that governments must decentralize their organizational structure in order to effectively provide citizens with access to the wide range of health, educational, environmental, cultural and economic services they need. In Burkina Faso, the national government is working with municipal authorities to improve local information and knowledge about the citizenry and the services they need and want. The responsibilities for providing various social services have been decentralized, and an information system is being developed to help with both funding and monitoring this decentralized structure.

Human Resources

Human resource management involves the planning, implementation and monitoring of the organization's labor force. Another way of looking at the organization's human resources is in terms of "human capital," which refers to the knowledge and skills of the labor force. Clearly, the human resources of any organization are its most valuable assets. In the view of many top-level executives, employees are the key source of an organization's competitive advantage (Brown and Kraft, 1998; Chilton, 1994).

Critically important to effective human resource management is to develop and instill core values throughout the organization (Down, Mardis, Connolly and Johnson, 1997). These values include integrity and honesty, commitment to the organizational mission, accountability for and pride in one's work, commitment to excellence, and building trust. They form the basis for developing cohesiveness and teamwork, as well as for developing policies, procedures and programs that focus on meeting the needs of customers or clients.

The human resources management function is charged with planning and controlling human resources to make sure that people's needs are met so they can work to achieve organizational goals. Commitment to meeting employees' needs is not merely an altruistic function—it is highly likely that staff who are reasonably comfortable with working conditions, and stimulated by the environment, will be productive (Miron, Leichtman and Atkins, 1993).

In traditional government bureaucracies, many human resource functions are centralized in a ministry and often not in the control of individual organizational bureaucracies. Increasingly, however, as part of overall public sector reforms, government ministries and agencies are taking control of some of these functions. From an organizational perspective, control over human resources is critical to hold managers accountable for organizational performance. Nevertheless, progress in this area has been slow.

The following sections examine five aspects of human resources management: planning, staffing, developing, assessing and rewarding, and maintaining effective relations.

Human Resources Planning

Human resources planning involves forecasting the human resources needs of the organization, and planning the steps necessary to meet these needs. This planning is the first step in any effective human resources management function. Human resources planning should be closely linked to the organization's strategic objectives and mission. Even in regions of the world with a plentiful, well-educated workforce, such planning is a challenge because the needs of the organization are constantly changing and sometimes do not converge (Cockerill, Hunt and Schroder, 1995).

The challenge is even greater if the pool of people from which the organization recruits is limited by such factors as brain drain, or because labor market wages in the private sector are more attractive (Colvard, 1994). Forecasting in these environments is quite difficult.

Questions: Planning

- To what extent does the organization's ability to plan for its human resources needs affect its performance?
- Are the right people in the right jobs in the organization?
- Can the organization forecast current and future demands for human resources?
- Does the organization know how and where to identify people with the skills needed to fill its needs?
- Can the organization link its mission and goals to its human resources planning?
- Has the organization developed a personnel policy manual?

Staffing Human Resources

An important step in implementing a human resources plan is to recruit and train new people to carry out the work of the organization. *Staffing an organization means searching for, selecting and orienting individuals who have the appropriate range of knowledge, skills, behavior and values to meet the organization's needs.*

Staffing also means responding to trends in the labor pools and helping people adjust to the environment within which the organization is operating.

Staffing capacity relates to the ability of an organization to identify the kinds of human resources that it needs to perform well (McNerney, 1995). It does this through a variety of techniques involved in job and needs assessments, review of core competencies, organizational human resource competency analysis, and so forth. An organization must find new organizational members who cannot only meet the present demand for human resource services, but also future needs.

HUMAN RESOURCE IMPLICATIONS OF SOCIAL TRENDS

- Increased pressure on employee benefits
- Need for increased multi-cultural management skills
- Growing emphasis on attracting and retaining skilled labor
- Policy development required regarding flextime
- Work design required to increase employee autonomy
- Policy development needed to take into account changing family structures
- Recruitment required to handle outsourcing and short-term contracting needs
- Need for participatory leadership skill development
- Organizational design skills required to increase decentralization

HUMAN RESOURCE IMPLICATIONS OF ECONOMIC TRENDS

- Downward pressure on costs increases focus on results of human resource initiatives
- Increased requirement for skills in "marrying" organizational cultures
- Rapid response required in assessing and reporting on skills inventory
- Increased need for skills for driving organizational design
- Need to focus on lifestyle benefits and working conditions for employees

HUMAN RESOURCE IMPLICATIONS OF POLITICAL TRENDS

- Increased need for human resources staff to have knowledge and expertise in interpreting and applying new human resource legislation

HUMAN RESOURCE IMPLICATIONS OF TECHNOLOGICAL TRENDS

- Increased technological skills required for all staff, including human resources staff
- Job redesign to address demands for telecommuting
- Redesign of management process to manage telecommuters
- Just-in-time training
- More skills needed to analyze and synthesize information for staff at most levels

It is a sobering thought to think that in many government organizations the people being hired today could very well be the workers 20 to 30 years from now. While there are no guarantees with respect to how people will mature in their organizational role, initial selection and training play an important role in assuring good long-term performance.

Questions: Staffing

- *To what extent does the organization have adequate staffing procedures to ensure that it knows the type of staff required for high performance?*
- *Does the organization have a competent approach to staffing?*
- *Does the organization have appropriate job descriptions, competency reviews or equivalents to determine what staffing is needed?*
- *Does the organization have an appropriate system for selecting candidates (reviewing curriculum vitae, conducting interviews, and checking references)?*
- *Are individuals in charge of selection appropriately trained to carry out this function (interview and listening skills, courtesy, and good judgment)?*
- *Is recruitment and selection material (ads, posting, interview questions) free of discrimination (gender, religious)? Is it transparent?*
- *Is there someone familiar with both the day-to day functions of the organization as well as its longer-term vision available to orient new staff members?*

Developing Human Resources

Building human resource skills, knowledge and attitudes is becoming an increasingly important part of the work of an organization. In a period of rapid change, the staff of an organization needs to adapt to changing conditions (Bennett, 1993). For example, public servants today need to know how to work with a wide variety of stakeholders. In the manufacturing sector, new technologies have revolutionized the production of goods. In almost every aspect of work today, employees need to adapt, change and learn. This is the human resource development function of an organization.

Developing human resources in an organization means improving employee performance by increasing or improving their skills, knowledge and attitudes. This allows the organization to remove or prevent performance deficiencies, makes employees more flexible and adaptable, and increases staff commitment to the organization. Developing human resources can take several forms, such as job training, training for the role inside the organization, or training for a career. This can include career development, succession planning, or organizational development activities. Having the right people skills in place at the right time is an important aspect of the human resource development system.

An effective and popular approach to develop human capital is staff training and development programs (Harrison, 1997). The basic purpose of such programs is to enable employees to acquire the requisite knowledge and skills that will upgrade their job performance. Management training and development programs can facilitate the development of skills and communication among staff by providing a common language, building employee networks, and establishing a common vision for the firm. These programs promote cohesion by helping employees socialize, instilling in them a common set of core values, and improving employee skills critical to the organization's key operations and its core and distinctive competencies (Hagen, Hassan and Amin, 1998).

Historically in development work, there has been a great deal of investment in training. In many development projects, training as part of technical assistance is perceived as a panacea for poor individual performance. It is easy to disburse for training activities and it is also easy to obtain visible outputs. As such, it is a fairly safe tactic. Unfortunately, training may not be the most appropriate intervention for improving employee productivity and, hence, organizational performance. Many

---

TRAINING ALONE DOES NOT ALWAYS SOLVE PROBLEMS

Developing human resources in organizations through education and training is a popular way to address identified organizational needs. However, addressing a training need of an individual might not address the underlying organizational problem.

For most of the 1980s and into the 1990s, donors attempted to upgrade the performance of the airports of the Leeward and Windward Islands. This required improving airport maintenance systems, upgrading navigational aids, and undertaking institutional and infrastructure development. Since new technologies were used in upgrading navigational equipment and computerization of various airport functions, training and staff development were clearly an integral part of the intervention.

A review of lessons learned indicated that training was most successful when it was part of an integrated set of activities and included incentives to encourage staff to use it on the job (Universalia, 1991). In particular, performance associated with the use of new navigational aids was enhanced when institutional policy, organizational (decentralization of authority) and individual changes (performance reviews) were made.

observers doubt that training is an effective way to improve performance in developing countries because it is often isolated and not linked to infrastructure, job requirements, incentive structures or evaluation procedures. Furthermore, in many developing countries, training becomes the means by which staff leave the civil service. Care and balance, then, clearly must be exercised.

Questions: Developing Human Resources

- To what extent does the organization have an overall approach to human resource development?
- Does the organization have a training and development policy?
- Does it have a budget for training and development and a way to track these costs?
- Does the organization encourage staff to continue to learn and develop (by providing incentives for learning, by supporting training costs)?
- Is there someone in the organization able to identify training needs?
- Does the organization support the application and transfer of new learning on the job?
- Is training demand driven (responds to needs in the organization) as opposed to supply driven (responds to whatever is offered on the market or by a donor)?
- Can and does the organization assess training and its effect on performance?
- Does the organization have plans for mentoring younger staff into their careers?
- Does the organization have a way to deal with succession?
- Do people see career opportunities in the organization?

Assessing and Rewarding Human Resources

An important aspect of the human resources management function is the system and approach the organization uses to collect information and provide feedback to individuals or teams. This means assessing the contribution of each staff member to distribute rewards (direct and indirect, monetary and non-monetary) within the legal regulations of the region and the organization's ability to pay. The assessment and reward system should help the organization retain good employees, motivate staff, administer pay within legal regulations, facilitate organizational strategic objectives, and support individual learning.

The evaluation and incentive system is a key component in an organizational analysis and is associated with overall organizational performance. Many issues

WHAT IS THE "RIGHT" INCENTIVE SYSTEM?

One of the big problems in the public service of developing countries is how to assess and appropriately compensate staff for normal or exceptional performance. This is a complex issue for many reasons. First, it is often difficult to identify objective performance criteria for many civil service jobs, which can require a tradeoff of control (making sure people deserve government service) and the actual provision of service. It is also difficult to create rating systems for jobs that are fair and equitable. Historically, work dominated by women in teaching and nursing paid less than other government work that required less training and often less responsibility.

In some governments, there is a need to make subtle judgments. For example, food licensing requires protection of both the public as well as the service aspect. Which should be rewarded? In addition, in many developing as well as developed countries, government unions have not embraced merit or performance pay schemes. The difficulty with not having adequate incentive systems is that the employees themselves create the system.

must be addressed when looking at these components. With respect to assessing staff, an organizational approach is needed that links the needs of the organization and the demands of the job. The incentive and reward structures within an organization are complex to understand and address. There are both monetary and non-monetary rewards that interact as rewards (and punishments) in all organizations.

Questions: Assessing and Rewarding

- To what extent does the organization have fair and motivational assessment and reward systems?
- Does the organization have a compensation policy that complies with the rules and regulations of the country?
- Does the staff see an adequate correlation between compensation and performance?
- Are staff members generally satisfied with their compensation?
- Are compensation packages externally competitive for the sector?
- Is there internal equity in salaries and benefits (i.e., equal compensation for work of equal value)?
- Are compensation differentials appropriate to motivate staff?
- Does the organization motivate staff with both monetary and non-monetary rewards?

Individuals make choices based on their understanding of these incentives about whether to work or not, how hard to work, and so forth (Gerhart and Milkovich, 1990).

Not everyone is motivated by the same rewards. Some people are motivated by money, others less so. Some want prestigious titles or positions, while others could care less. In some organizations, weak incentives lead to absences or corruption. In countries with more powerful labor unions, weak incentives can affect relations with unions and even cause strikes. With respect to this area of analysis, it is worth trying to understand both the visible and underlying patterns of the organization.

Maintaining Effective Staff Relations

Keeping a supportive and content work force is becoming more important in this era of global competition. Today, it is increasingly difficult to find people with the right skills at the right price. When an organization trains its staff, it is investing in future productivity. Creating the work and support structures to retain a loyal work force is difficult, but important, for an organization. *This aspect of the human resources function deals with all the programs and systems in place to ensure employees are protected and dealt with in accordance with appropriate legislation.* It includes all the activities the organization implements to address issues of health and safety, human rights, the quality of working conditions, and, in unionized settings, collective bargaining. In essence, it represents the concrete measures the organization has taken to instill in employees feel-

---

Questions: Staff Relations

- *To what extent does the organization have effective relations among its staff?*
- *Do people in the organization feel protected from being taken advantage of (through a collective agreement or appropriate personnel policies)?*
- *Are there measures and procedures inside the organization to deal with people in emotional or physical distress?*
- *Does the organization seek ways to increase the loyalty and commitment of staff?*
- *Is morale in the organization generally good?*
- *Does the organization have measures in place to deal with harassment in the workplace?*
- *Does the organization have, if appropriate, a health and safety policy?*
- *Are work-related accidents rare?*

---

ings of ownership, self-control, responsibility and self-respect. Exactly what the organization does to produce these outcomes will vary according to the nature of the organization, its leadership style, and its cultural setting.

FINANCIAL MANAGEMENT

Management of an organization's financial resources is a critical capacity. Good management of budgeting, financial record keeping and reporting is essential to the overall functioning of the organization (Berry et al., 1985). It ensures that the board of directors and the managers have the information they need to make decisions and allocate organizational resources. It also inspires confidence in funders interested in financial accountability and sound financial management (Goddard and Powell, 1994). *Financial management involves the planning, implementation and monitoring of the monetary resources of an organization. Along with human resources, it provides the major inputs upon which an organization builds its products and services.*

The people responsible for the organization's financial management need to plan and budget resources (operating and capital budgets), handle cash management, and manage accounting and financial reporting. The board and senior managers should be involved in financial management and be clear about accountability. The organization also requires skilled people at both the board and staff levels to carry out the financial analysis and work (Birkin and Woodward, 1997).

Financial statements, including the balance sheet and income statements, are barometers of organizational health. Sound internal financial procedures regarding the administration of the organization's operating funds and individual program grants offer assurance that monies are directed properly. Overall, important organizational goals should be supported by the budget. For example, if the international exchange of information is one of the organization's priorities, the budget should allocate funds for electronic data systems, hosting international visitors, and other activities related to supporting this goal.

Financial management includes financial planning, financial accountability, and financial statements and systems, all of which will be discussed individually in this section. Building a transparent financial system with competent staff helps many countries fight corruption.

Financial Planning

Organizations require resources to operate. Financial resources are needed to pay both the short- and long-term expenses incurred by an organization (Schick, 1993). To ensure there is enough money available, the organization must:

- Predict its anticipated operating expenses
- Determine the amount of funds required for capital expenditures
- Predict when and how much cash is required over a period of time

Financial planning is the organization's ability to forecast its future monetary needs and requirements. This involves a variety of forecasting tools. In the government sector, an organization needs to estimate its committed operating expenses, as well as any new activities it plans to engage in. Because governments usually charge most capital costs in the year they occur (they do not use the idea of depreciation), they also need to plan for fully costing capital expenditures (Goddard and Powell, 1994).

By contrast, private sector organizations and most NGOs need to determine the revenues they anticipate from the sale of their goods or services Within this context,

---

Questions: Financial Planning

- Is regular and periodic financial planning undertaken to support performance?
- Is there adequate budgetary planning?
- Are cash requirements analyzed through cash flow statements?
- Are budget plans timely?
- Are budget plans updated as financial information comes in?
- Are members of the governing body involved in financial planning and monitoring?
- Are human resources adequate to ensure effective financial planning?
- Is the financing of grants or loans properly managed?
- Are comparisons of both actual and planned budgets monitored and analyzed for decision-making?
- Are there appropriate capital and equipment forecasts?
- Are reports provided to senior managers, the board and funders on a regular basis (at least once a quarter)?
- Is financial information provided in a timely fashion to those who need it?

if they are able to borrow long-term funds from the market, they can purchase capital equipment in the present year and not fully pay for it until later.

However, determining the resources available is not the only planning required by organizations. Both public and private agencies need to determine when they will have the cash to pay for the expenses they incur. Forecasting cash requirements is a challenging endeavor for both private and public organizations.

The ability to plan revenues and cash requirements provides a framework within which an organization can make decisions about present and future program and capital needs. The organization's financial planning should include both its short- and long-term financial requirements, along with its need for cash.

Financial Accountability

Keeping track of financial resources is one of the more structured aspects of organizational life. In most government and private organizations, there are procedures that govern the request and use of financial resources. Normally, organizational members cannot draw on the financial resources of an organization unless they follow established rules and obtain the various required approvals. The basis of financial accountability is the ability to account for the use of resources provided to an organization (Birkin and Woodward, 1997; Schick, 1993).

Taking care of and accounting for the finances of the organization are prerequisites for external trust. This normally occurs within a highly structured, rule-based sys-

---

Questions: Financial Accountability

- Do members of the organization follow clearly stated financial procedures?
- Are the auditors satisfied with the organization's controls on cash and assets?
- Is there a clearly stated rule setting when the organizational year begins and ends?
- Does the board of directors review financial policies and procedures on a regular basis to assess whether they are adequate, inadequate or excessive?
- Are there competent staff and board members who understand the role of financial procedures and information?
- Is the financial information contextualized within a strategic or business plan?
- Is there a board committee to oversee financial issues? A management committee?

tem that is transparent and verified through various monitoring procedures (see next section). The structure of rules and transparency is operationalized by standard documents that need to be filled out and approved at various levels of an organization. It is by following these rules and approval procedures that accountability is developed.

Many organizations are pejoratively called "bureaucratic" because of the rule-based culture that surrounds their financial accountability. How many rules and regulations does an organization need to be accountable? How many approval signatures are required to act? All organizations need the appropriate checks and balances, but when are there too few of these, and when are they too many? Creating accountable financial systems is a crucial function for those internal and external professionals overseeing the care of organizational assets (Goddard and Powell, 1994).

Financial Monitoring

Financial monitoring involves the development and creation of timely reports so that managers can make timely financial decisions. Reporting of financial information has changed considerably in recent years. Twenty years ago, public sector managers and most not-for-profit organizations would expect to receive systematic information from their financial systems every three months. Organizational reviews typically recommended providing management with quarterly financial information. Today, the computerization of the financial function allows government agencies to obtain reports once a month, and in some private sector firms once a day, or even more frequently (Booth, 1996).

The forecasting of financial needs provides a framework for management. However, managers also need to know whether they are meeting, exceeding or failing to meet their projections, so that they may make the necessary adjustments required. The financial managers of the organization are responsible for the preparation, timeliness, integrity and objectivity of its financial statements. At a minimum, this means there must be regular financial reports generated from the bookkeeping system.

To cite one example, whereas private schools throughout the world always managed their own financial systems, this was not the case for public schools. In the public sector, school principals in general were bureaucrats carrying out the educational process of the country or the will of the party in power, or alternatively, attempting to exercise some management or leadership over what was being taught. However, as educational systems become decentralized, school principals have found themselves having to monitor the financial aspects of schooling and report to external entities, such as a governing council. In this context, and increasingly in other decentralized contexts such as health and municipalities, public sector managers are having to set up financial systems that allow them to regularly report how to manage the financial assets entrusted to them. Historically, this function was centralized and was among their responsibilities.

Thus, the monitoring of financial information plays an increasingly important role in the work of all public sector managers. It is also one of the areas most often inserted into loan agreements.

Questions: Financial Monitoring

- Are there financial reports and statements to support effective decision-making and good performance?
- Is there an adequate bookkeeping system that can generate monitoring information?
- Is there adequate staff to record financial information and generate reports?
- Are balance sheets and income and expense statements prepared on a timely basis (at least quarterly)?
- Are there adequate reports that allow for control of the organization's assets?
- Are cash flow statements prepared in timely fashion and used by managers?
- Is cash managed so that the organization can benefit when there is surplus, and minimize the cost of cash shortages?

INFRASTRUCTURE

While human resources and financial resources are quite typically reviewed in most organizational assessments, more attention needs to be paid in developing countries to the state of the infrastructure required to support organizational performance (Nourzad, 1997).

Infrastructure refers to the basic conditions (facilities and technology) that allow an organization's work to proceed—for example, reasonable space in a building equipped with adequate lighting, clean water and a dependable supply of electricity, as well as viable transportation to and from work for employees. In developed countries that have the wealth and the governmental structures to support adequate infrastructure, these conditions are often taken for granted. In some developing countries, however, inadequate infrastructure presents an organizational problem that warrants assessment.

Each organization has its own assets and liabilities with respect to infrastructure resources. If the organization has its basic infrastructure in place, this area will represent a small component of the assessment. If the infrastructure is deteriorated, however, with electricity and water found to be problem areas, then infrastructure will become a major concern of the assessment.

Facilities

People (staff, clients, customers) spend a lot of time in their organizational surroundings. Some surroundings exude the spirit of performance and development. Others are just the opposite.

As part of understanding the organization's capacity, it is necessary to consider the extent to which facilities support or interfere with the functioning or the potential functioning of the organization. Although single deficiencies in one or more elements of infrastructure may not interfere with day-to-day work, at some point, work will be affected. Typically, the basis of many infrastructure problems is maintenance, which often suffers due to the lack of a recurrent budget for upkeep.

Questions: Facilities

- Is the infrastructure adequate to support performance?
- Does the organizational strategy identify the opportunities and constraints regarding infrastructure?
- Are the buildings and internal services (water, electricity) adequate to support and facilitate daily work?
- Is there an adequate transportation system to and from work for employees?
- Are communications systems (hardware) functioning at the level required?
- Are there adequate maintenance systems and procedures supported by an ongoing maintenance budget?
- Is such infrastructure as building and equipment maintenance managed effectively and efficiently?
- Is there an individual or group responsible for adequate planning to address ongoing infrastructure concerns?

Technology

Globalization and information and communication technologies are creating a new information society paradigm of economic growth, citizen action, and political liberty. The information revolution is happening everywhere, often in haphazard fashion. Information and communication technologies have fundamentally altered the nature of global markets, transforming social and economic interactions, and redefining work (Gagnon and Dragon, 1996).

Technological change is occurring faster than policies are able to respond. Information gaps continue to exist between the developed and developing world, with the potential to disenfranchise entire communities on the edge of the information revolution. What lies ahead is tremendous structural change, uncertainty and risk.

The technological resources of an organization encompass all of the equipment, machinery and systems (including the library, information systems hardware and software) that are essential for the organization to function properly. Still, the instruments of technology are merely tools for enhancing services and products: ideas must still inspire the technology.

Questions: Technology

- *To what extent do technological resources affect the organization's performance?*
- *Is there adequate technological planning?*
- *Overall, is the organization's level of technology appropriate to carry out its functions?*
- *Is any particular unit seriously lagging behind the others technologically?*
- *Is access to international information provided to all units through library and information management systems?*
- *Are there adequate systems and training in place for managing organizational technology?*
- *Are there adequate information technologies in place to manage the organization?*

PROGRAM MANAGEMENT

According to Booth (1998), the term "program management" is used mainly by two groups of professionals in ways that are consistent. The first group, those involved with information systems, employs the term to describe the management of *big proj-*

ects, especially system implementations. The second group, corporate strategists, uses it to mean the *practical task of translating grand strategies into operational reality.*

In many organizations, individual managers typically pursue their own projects and cite their own successes. In fact, the link between their efforts and organizational performance is generally quite obscure. By coordinating and linking the cascade of corporate goals reflected in diverse projects into specific sets of common-goal actions, program management helps to avoid this problem. Program management is regarded as "an additional layer of management sitting above the projects and ensuring that they remain pertinent to the wider organization" (Booth, 1998).

In the context of funded organizations in developing countries, organizations often receive financing from different donors or funding agencies for different projects that are not necessarily congruent with organizational goals. In such a situation, there is a clear need for program management to align different projects with wider organizational goals and coordinate them into common-goal actions (see Box).

THE EFFECTS OF PROJECT MANAGEMENT

The purpose of the Rice Ecosystems Project was to explore the health impacts of irrigated rice production in West Africa, the research domain of the West Africa Rice Development Association (WARDA). The project was unusual, as it was the first time that WARDA, or any agricultural research center in the Consultative Group on International Agricultural Research (CGIAR), focused on the impact of its work on health. The project, therefore, required collaboration with a new group of health scientists, as well as the incorporation of the social sciences. There has been strong interest in the project across the consultative group system, and it is frequently noted as a pioneer in integrating social issues into agricultural research.

The project was overseen by an external technical committee that reviewed and endorsed the research protocols, ensuring a high standard of research. An evaluation was mandated to assess the financial viability of multi-disciplinary research at WARDA (that is, the relative costs of the studies), and the relevance of the research. What are the implications of the findings for the agricultural research and development sector? How was relevance achieved? What are the implications for future work?.

The evaluation also assessed the extent to which the Rice Ecosystems Project was supporting or limiting the performance of WARDA. The major question was how much the project coincided with WARDA's mission and goals. Was it stretching the organization beyond its mandate? This was critical, because a successful project could put the organization at risk if its purpose was too far removed from the group's mission.

Program management is vitally connected with the perceived quality of an organization. Organizations are known for, and gain their reputations from, their ability to provide appropriate goods and services. With respect to other aspects of organizational capacity, the perceived strength of an organization's strategic leadership, structure, human resources, financial resources, infrastructure, process management and inter-organizational linkages is linked to the quality of its programs. Program management ensures that proper weight is given to each facet of the organization's mission. Strategy and program management interact to make possible the attainment of overall organizational goals. It is useful for an organization to evaluate programs by assessing them in terms of their overall contribution to organizational performance.

Good program management requires a cycle of careful planning, implementation and evaluation. All programs go through this either formally or informally. Each of these aspects of good program management is discussed in the sections that follow.

Program Planning

Program planning ranges from working out what to do on a day-by-day basis to long-term strategic planning. It should be happening constantly within a project and pro-

---

Questions: Program Planning

- To what extent does the organization appropriately plan its programs?
- Is there a written plan for each program area and each major project?
- Are program and project plans linked to the organizational mission?
- Is there adequate program planning and budget programming to ensure that programs support the mission?
- Are programs and projects consistent with the mission, needs, strategies and priorities of the organization?
- Does program planning take into account technological, economic, gender, social and environmental aspects to ensure the applicability of programs?
- Are there adequate timelines?
- Are there adequate budgets?
- Is there adequate analysis of roles and responsibilities?
- Is there a procedure outlined to monitor results?

gram. Program planning must take into account what an organization has to do to create its goods and services, as well as the resources it needs to do so.

Program planning requires thinking ahead and, as such, involves several concurrent questions. Whom are we serving? What demand are we supplying and at what cost? What are our objectives? What must be done to meet these objectives? Who will do this? How will they do it? How long will it take? How much will it cost? How will we know whether we have met our objectives?

Program planning has many levels and is time bound, so it can be short, medium or long term. However, when conducting an assessment, the extent to which the organization's plans are well communicated and used as management tools must be determined. This will require written plans.

Program Implementation

The major task of managers is to put the organization's program into practice. It is all well and good to have a great plan—making it work is the hard part. Program implementation requires organization and having staff who can put their skills to work. It requires integration of the management skills needed to allocate resources and the technical skills needed to do what has to be done (for example, to provide

---

Questions: Program Implementation

- To what extent does the organization appropriately implement its programs?
- Does staff support the process of carrying out programs and delivering products and services to clients and beneficiaries?
- Are there good relationships among the staff who provide the products and services?
- Does staff work together to provide good products and services?
- Does the program team have good problem-solving skills?
- Are health and safety for staff and clients always a priority in implementation?
- Are resources efficiently used to provide the product or service?
- Are time schedules adhered to in a reasonable fashion?
- Is staff motivated to work together to get things done?
- Are program meetings productive?

---

health services and do research). Program implementation is the stage at which an organization integrates all its resources to concretely achieve its goals.

Program Monitoring and Evaluation

Programs are central to the life of an organization. Management needs to keep track of them to ensure they are meeting their objectives and achieving their intended results. Similarly, oversight agencies need to have the means to track the results of public programs.[1] Sound project monitoring and evaluation need to be built into projects during their planning stage and carried out throughout the project (IDB, 1997).

For example, an assessment of the evaluability of a program or project ensures that it contains the basic elements required to monitor results and ultimately determine whether development objectives are being met. In the planning section, we suggest that there are an increasing array of tools that help project planners develop quality projects. The logical framework can be incorporated into a project both

---

Questions: Program Monitoring and Evaluation

- To what extent does the organization monitor its programs appropriately?
- Are monitoring and evaluation systems in place?
- Is program staff given feedback on program performance?
- Are there adequate opportunities to clarify roles and responsibilities?
- Are there adequate opportunities to review program indicators to measure progress against plans?
- Are timelines monitored to reduce overruns?
- Are budgets reviewed in a timely fashion?
- Are programs reviewed on a regular basis with respect to how they contribute to the overall organizational strategy?
- Are lessons encouraged?
- Are corrective actions taken when difficulties arise?
- Are monitoring and evaluation seen as ongoing and normal processes?

---

[1] See U.S. General Accounting Office (1998) for information on monitoring and evaluating the program plans of government agencies.

for use as a planning tool but also to provide indicators for monitoring and evalua-tion (IDB, 1997). Similarly, outcome mapping (Earl, Carden and Smutylo, 2001) is used as a tool to support better planning, monitoring and evaluation.

PROCESS MANAGEMENT

Executives with many organizations today view their business as a series of func-tional silos concerned with their own requirements (Dent and Hughes, 1998). This perspective is particularly pervasive among managers accustomed to being reward-ed for optimizing the performance of their functions relative to the rest of the organ-ization. Although managers talk about "big picture" processes, their efforts are often focused inwardly on their own requirements and are measured accordingly. In such situations, there is an obvious need for common systems and operations that apply uniformly throughout the organization and, like a thread, sew the various function-al parts together into a common purpose. There is also a need for compatible strate-gies to optimize organizational performance.

In other words, process management is required.

Taking a vision and making it a reality through smooth-flowing daily work in an organization is largely dependent on ongoing "processes." These are the internal value-adding management systems and operations that cut across functional and departmental boundaries. They are the mechanisms that guide interactions among all groups of people in an organization to ensure that ongoing work is accomplished rather than hindered or blocked.

Thus, *process management is the task of aligning and integrating the various practices and cultures of different segments of an organization through the introduction of common systems and operations that apply uniformly to all segments of the organization.* These common operations or processes include problem-solving, planning, decision-making, communication, and monitoring and evaluation.

People often interact to accomplish their work, and the way that organizational processes are set up dictates the tone of their interaction. If the processes are all work-ing, the outcome is that the organization is learning and accomplishing a great deal.

Process management takes place at every level of an organization, from the board of directors to the line worker. The board and senior managers must know how to problem-solve, plan and make timely decisions. If they are deficient in these areas, organizational direction is often hampered. At the more operational level, program units, departments and other functional segments of the organization must plan and set short- and medium-term goals, as well as solve problems, make decisions and generate strategies to carry out appropriate activities to achieve results.

Problem-solving

Problem-solving is probably the most universal or prevalent of all thinking activities. As individuals, we spend each day of our lives solving problems: deciding what to eat and what to wear, what needs to be done first and what can be put off until tomorrow. At this level, problem-solving skills become programmed or automated over time, and we rarely think about them.

At the organizational level, similar problems constantly confront every unit or department. How can we increase our revenues? Should a new product be introduced? Should more or fewer workers be employed? How can production costs be cut down without compromising quality? How can we best sell our products or services? Who should do what and when?

Disparities in problem-solving approaches, which determine how well opportunities are capitalized on, partly explains why some organizations are so successful at improving their performance, while others struggle. All the other activities in process management—decision-making, planning, and monitoring and evaluation—are part of the problem-solving process.

Questions: Problem-solving

- Does the work at various levels of the organization flow smoothly, or is it blocked? If blocked, is an inadequate problem-solving process the cause?
- Has the real problem been diagnosed?
- Is the problem clearly defined?
- Is it possible that perception biases have distorted problem identification?
- Is the problem well structured, straightforward and familiar? Or is it a new or unusual problem regarding which information is ambiguous or incomplete?
- Are adequate organizational problem-solving skills found on the governing board and within the ranks of senior managers?
- Are problem-solving techniques adequate in departments and for important projects?

The first step in a systematic approach to problem-solving is to identify or understand the problem and define it clearly. Sometimes, diagnosing a critical problem in time is the difference between survival and extinction. Often, what is perceived as "the problem" may only be a symptom of a much bigger and deep-seated problem. Therefore, *successfully diagnosing the root problem and clearly defining it becomes the first prerequisite to removing bottlenecks and taking the organization in the right direction.* Once the exact problem is identified and defined, the next step is to devise alternative ways of solving it. This takes us into the realm of decision-making.

Decision-making

Decision-making is the process of selecting from among alternative courses of action generated during the problem-solving process. Decision-making is:

■ Programmed: a repetitive decision that can be handled by a routine approach;
■ Procedural: a series of interrelated steps used to respond to a structured problem;
■ Rule-based: depends on an explicit statement that tells managers what they ought or ought not to do;
■ Policy-based: provides a guide that establishes parameters for selecting among alternative courses of action.[2]

Questions: Decision-making

■ *Do all segments of the organization have adequate decision-making skills?*
■ *Is enough information available on all alternative courses of action?*
■ *Can the degree of certainty or uncertainty associated with the correctness of the decision be reasonably estimated?*
■ *In a situation of uncertainty, what are the consequences of making the wrong decision?*
■ *Are decisions made in a timely manner?*
■ *Are decisions made by groups?*

---

[2] See the Web site at http://www.rrtrade.org/classes/decision/rational/tsl001.htm

Decision-making is often influenced or even constrained by limits to decision-makers' information processing capacity, as well as their background, position in the organization, interests, and experiences. In this context, group decisions, although time consuming, may have significant advantages over individual decisions, since they can lead to more diverse and complete information, and can increase the legitimacy and acceptance of the proposed course of action.

Planning

Planning is the process of mapping where you are going and how you will get there. It permeates every activity of a successful organization, from product or service initiation to production, selling and distribution. In a world that is ever more complex and uncertain, the adage that "failing to plan is planning to fail" is now truer than ever. Planning helps predict how organizational members will behave. The strategic plan sets an organization's overall direction and, at operational levels, becomes the process by which strategy is translated into specific objectives and methodologies to accomplish goals. It involves optimally engaging resources, time and people by developing timelines and work schedules.

Policies and procedures are special types of plans that set out courses of action for members of the organization. Generally, the degree to which plans, procedures and policies are explicit varies considerably across organizations, and even within a particular organization. Organization members need enough direction to know what to do to support the organization's mission and goals. The planning of policies and procedures should provide this direction adequately at all levels of the organization; that is, for projects, for departments, and for the organization as a whole.

Questions: Planning

- *Is there adequate, inadequate or excessive planning and policy procedure development in the organization at all levels (from the governing board to departments and individual projects)?*
- *Is the process of planning contributing to the strategic direction of the organization?*
- *Do plans provide adequate direction to organizational members?*
- *Are plans, policies and procedures generally followed? Why or why not?*

Communication

Communication is the process by which information is exchanged and shared understanding is achieved among members of an organization. The top-down and bottom-up flow of information is a vital process that can facilitate or hinder the smooth functioning of an organization. It includes both the formal and informal flow of information.

Internal communication can serve as the glue holding an organization together. Alternatively, it can break it apart, for both information and misinformation constantly flow in organizations. Accurate information provided through a system of top-down flows and feedback is vital to keep employees aware about what needs to be done, and to keep managers informed about what was achieved.

An effective internal communication system also helps to motivate employees, for apart from the specific information needed to carry out work, organization members also need information that makes them feel they are part of an important effort and a wider purpose. The organization must create mechanisms that help its members have access to both types of information. Coordinating committees, working groups, debriefing sessions, newsletters and meetings of all sorts are the vehicles through which effective communication is achieved within an organization. (Communication with external constituents is dealt with in the next section on inter-organizational linkages.)

Questions: Communication

- Are there adequate channels for top-down and bottom-up flows of information?
- What are the main vehicles of internal communication?
- Do staff members feel that there is adequate and ongoing communication about the organization's activities?
- Do staff members receive information related to the organizational mission and progress in fulfilling the mission?
- If information circulated about activities becomes distorted, are there corrective mechanisms to remedy this?
- Do people have easy access to those in the organization with whom they must deal? Can they communicate easily with them?

Organizational Monitoring and Evaluation

Organizational monitoring and evaluation complement program monitoring and evaluation. Organizational monitoring can help clarify program objectives, link activities and inputs to those objectives, set performance targets, collect routine data, and feed results directly to those responsible. Monitoring is the ongoing, systematic processes of self-assessment.

Organizational evaluation looks at why and how results were or were not achieved at the organizational level. It links specific activities to overall results, includes broader outputs that are not readily quantifiable, explores unintended results, and provides overall lessons that can help adjust programs and policies to improve results.

Questions: Organizational Monitoring and Evaluation

- *Is adequate monitoring and evaluation occurring to improve performance?*
- *Are there policies and procedures that guide evaluation and monitoring?*
- *Are resources assigned to monitoring and evaluation?*
- *Are monitoring and evaluation valued at all levels of the organization as ways to improve performance?*
- *Are data obtained and used to monitor and evaluate the organization's units and activities?*
- *Are the data gathered through organizational monitoring and evaluation activities utilized?*
- *Do evaluation plans or performance monitoring frameworks exist?*
- *Are evaluation results mentioned in strategy, program, policy and budgetary documents?*
- *Do people have skills to monitor and evaluate?*
- *Are monitoring and evaluation valued processes?*
- *Are lessons learned from monitoring and evaluation, and do changes occur as a result?*

INTER-ORGANIZATIONAL LINKAGES

Having regular contact with other institutions, organizations and groups of strategic importance to the organization's work can result in a healthy exchange of approaches and resources (including knowledge and expertise). The organization may be forming or already have linkages with potential collaborators and collegial bodies, potential funders, or key constituents (Grandori, 1997).

Linkages help the organization keep up with advances in pertinent fields, and give access to wide-ranging sources of up-to-date information within each area of the organization's work (Coyne and Dye, 1998).

Today, there are many types of organizational arrangements that can and need to be made to support the organization's performance. For example, new information technologies can help an organization learn about the most recent approaches to programming and managerial issues. They also bring new ways to communicate with potential allies and collaborators in key program and funding areas. Two aspects of inter-organizational linkages are discussed in this section: new forms of relationships (such as networks, joint ventures, partnerships and coalitions), and electronic linkages.

Networks, Joint Ventures, Coalitions and Partnerships

While electronic linkages are opening organizations to new ideas and ways of communicating, a similar revolution is occurring with respect to new organizational patterns that support joint work and collaboration (Lorenzoni and Baden-Fuller, 1995).

Many organizations find that they are unable to move toward their mission without the help and support of like-minded organizations. Many are forming new types of relationships (either formal or informal) with other organizations to support their desire to be more successful.

Networks are an informal type of linkage that involves loosely coupled groups that are linked together to serve common interests. At the more formal end are the new partnerships,

---

Questions: Networks, Joint Ventures, Coalitions and Partnerships

- *Are external linkages adequately established or pursued to support performance?*
- *Does the organization have adequate formal and informal linkages with like-minded organizations?*
- *Are institutional linkages adequately supported?*
- *Do institutional linkages contribute efficiently to the organization's goals and mission?*
- *Are there fruitful and ongoing partnerships with external organizations that bring new ideas and resources to the organization?*
- *Is the organization communicating information about its work to external stakeholders, including the general public?*

coalitions and joint ventures. The most formal relationships are based on contractual agreements. All of these new linkages are breaking down the boundaries of organizations and are changing the way they operate.

Electronic Linkages

Electronic linkages are a worldwide assembly of systems, including communication networks, information equipment, information resources, and people of all skill levels and backgrounds. In other words, they represent a "network of networks."

Organizational capacity and performance increases through the appropriate use of new electronic technologies. These new technologies have the potential to improve communication and keep people informed about the latest ideas in the field. Organizational members can join discussion groups and other electronic mechanisms that link people of like minds and ideas. Electronic systems provide the opportunity to search the entire globe for new ideas and information, unlimited access to public services, cultural opportunities, commercial transactions, etc. (Lorenzoni and Baden-Fuller, 1995).

Questions: Electronic Linkages

- *Are external technological linkages adequately established or pursued to support the organization's performance?*
- *Is the organization electronically linked to the external world of colleagues, clients and markets (users) in such a way that these relationships are active and beneficial?*
- *Are electronic networks supported financially and technically?*
- *Do electronic networks effectively respond to the needs, shared interests and capabilities of the organization?*
- *Do electronic networks support new efficiency practices?*
- *Are there fruitful and ongoing partnerships with external organizations that bring new ideas and resources to the organization?*
- *Is the organization communicating information about its work to external stakeholders, including the general public?*
- *Do electronic linkages afford organizations the privacy and security required for day-to-day transactions?*
- *Will electronic linkages support existing trade barriers and any other controls?*

Chapter Four

ORGANIZATIONAL MOTIVATION

As we developed our approach to analyzing organizations, it became apparent to us that organizations, like people, have different personalities and work in different rhythms. We were often surprised at how well some organizations seem to work under incredibly difficult circumstances, while others are continually failing to perform under much more favorable conditions. Why? And why do people in some organizations seem to throw themselves at their work with tremendous zeal, while in others, they come to work and do as little as possible? Why is it that some organizations have a vision that puts them in the forefront of innovation, while others are always lagging behind, not knowing where they are going? The ideas associated with organizational motivation help provide insight into why organizations and the people inside them behave the way they do.

For almost a century now, organizational analysts have pondered the issue of why some individuals are more motivated than others (Maslow, 1997). A great deal can be learned from this literature about the types of working conditions that support or hinder how individuals in organizations perform. Only over the past 20 years has interest shifted from simply understanding the individual's role in organizational motivation, to some of the underlying personality aspects of the organization itself (Bloor and Dawson, 1994).

Although organizational motivation is manifested in a variety of ways, four primary concepts provide insight into the underlying personality of most organizations: history, mission, culture and incentives.

The first concept is the history and life cycle of the organization. Organizations, like people, vary in the different stages of their organizational life (Gupta and Chin, 1994). When they start up, there is often a state of optimistic euphoria, a belief that the resources brought together can do just about anything. While there are not consistent stages in an organization's life that parallel the human life span, there are stages that help to diagnose the organization and its culture. New or young organizations create their own unique patterns of behavior that are normally more informal than formal. In these organizations, roles and responsibilities are not delineated, few policy manuals exist, neither rules nor procedures are established, and there is an excitement normally associated with a new endeavor.

Motivation in these organizations at this early stage is driven in part by the experimental atmosphere that prevails. New entrepreneurial leaders often emerge, and there is a feeling that almost anything is possible. However, as these organizations mature, they begin to develop structures and rules. People are no longer free to make up their own ways of doing things. Roles and responsibilities are set. The excitement of newness fades and other motivational patterns emerge. As the context of the organization changes, it becomes imperative for the organization to change. We talk about organizational renewal or rebirth. If organizations do not renew themselves they become ill, and in the private sector, at least, they die.

While the metaphor of the organizational life cycle does not strictly hold true, understanding the history of an organization gives insight into what the organization is. The organization's raison d'être, the characteristics of its founders, an understanding of its major milestones and organizational changes—all play an important role in shaping the personality of an organization and how it performs.

The second concept of motivation focuses on the role or purpose of the organization: its mission. Every organization has a distinct role or purpose that is manifested in its goals and objectives. In most definitions of the concept of "organization," there is an explicit goal orientation. Each organization creates, either implicitly or explicitly, a forward looking direction of what it wants to accomplish, a vision of where it wants to go, or what it wants to be (Allen, 1995). Some organizations are motivated by the opportunity to do good works or to provide services to citizens. Many NGOs are motivated by helping those in need. Other organizations, such as research centers, may be driven by prestige—the desire to be regarded as the best in their field. In the private sector, motivation might mean having a bigger market share. Organizational analysts recognize the important role mission plays in shaping and creating an organization's personality, and as such consider it an important diagnostic consideration. Analyzing the mission of an organization offers insights into the organization itself.

Culture, the third concept, also provides a window to view organizational motivation. Organizational culture relates to the shared assumptions, values and beliefs held by organizational members These factors are at work, however subliminally, within the organization's boundaries. The culture of an organization is rarely written down, but it is definitely communicated to members and stakeholders in a variety of formal and informal ways. Analyzing organizational culture is critical in trying to understand the motivational forces that support or oppose change and improved performance.

Finally, the personality of an organization is shaped by its incentive system. For an organization to perform well, it must have mechanisms that encourage individuals and groups to work toward both its short- and long-term interests. These may include tangible benefits such as salary and bonuses, or less tangible incentives such as the freedom to pursue interests, or to participate in collaborative initiatives. Over the years, many studies have attempted to better understand the needs of organizational members to develop improved or alternative reward structures. What are the incentive systems and what do they reward? Understanding an organization's incentive system is key to understanding its underlying personality (Gupta and Jenkins, 1996).

These four motivational variables are not necessarily independent of one another, nor are they necessarily the only factors that provide insight into the personality of an organization. Rather, they are simply important factors that help complete the picture of organizational performance and its underlying elements. The sections that follow explore the definitions and dimensions of these four concepts in greater detail, and look at how to go about examining them in the context of an organizational assessment.

History

Definition

An organization's history is charted in its important milestones—*the story of its inception, growth, awards and achievements, and notable changes in structure or leadership. But its history is told as well in its failures and near misses*—the disasters, the things that almost worked, and the hopes and aspirations of leaders who tried to take the organization into new areas but were unable to gain either internal or external support. And while the evolution of an organization is sometimes revealed in formal documents and plans (strategic or otherwise), it is more often and more eloquently recounted through the unwritten stories that weave their way through the organization's oral history.

Dimensions

Analysts notice patterns in the history of organizations. Since the early work of Haire (1956), the notion took hold that an organization's history can be understood as a life cycle—that organizations, like people, experience identifiable stages in their evolution. While these organizational stages do not have the same developmental imperative of the human life cycle, using the latter as a type of framework was helpful to organizational analysis. Each stage in an organization's life cycle has particular characteristics that help determine the underlying personality of the organization.

Basically, the life cycle of an organization encompasses a start-up or inception phase (birth), a period of growth and development (adolescence), a mature stage (adult), and, eventually, a stage of decline (old age). While these stages seem linear, organizations do not necessarily go through them in a linear fashion. Some organizations are constantly starting over after what might be termed "false starts," while others mature and start to decline and then re-engineer themselves into a new organization. The notion of a life cycle gives shape to understanding the evolution of an organization, its stages of adaptation and change, and why it is performing as it is (Gupta and Chin, 1994).

We reviewed an organization that worked with communities to reduce poverty, in part by obtaining and distributing food from donor countries. About 10 years old at the time of the assessment, the organization was quite successful in its early stages, but more recently was experiencing serious difficulties (see Box on page 89).

Birth

At the beginning of an organization's life, its personality is shaped by its newness. Everything and everyone is new and open to ideas. Everything needs to be created. Everything needs to be discovered by those working in the organization. How do we get things done? What is the best way to do this? In the early stages, there is often a leader who takes on a major portion of the responsibilities with respect to establishing the organization's role, its niche in the environment, the ways of working, and a way for the organization to financially survive. This is a period when the personality of the leader can have an immediate impact on the organization. Many organizations in the early stages of development have inspirational leaders with vision and ideas. To succeed, however, the organization must translate these ideas into action.

Typically, this phase is characterized by informal communications and structures. There are relatively few rules or procedures, and people invent ways to accomplish their

When we came in as external reviewers, we were told that the original founder and CEO of the organization to be assessed was a deeply religious man who had tremendous compassion for his staff and for the poor. Both the staff and community trusted the leader of the organization.

During the seventh year of the organization's existence, a major international donor was looking for an executing agency in Ethiopia to distribute food. The donor indicated to the organization that it would be willing to provide a substantial amount of grain if storage arrangements could be made for future distribution. The founder agreed, and the organization began the task of arranging to increase its grain storage capacity fourfold. To do this, it needed funds to build new grain storage facilities and increase its distribution system accordingly. In quadrupling its service potential, the organization needed management systems in order to operate the multimillion-dollar acquisition, storage, sale and distribution process. Although the founder was instrumental in getting the work off the ground, he was less successful in creating the management systems necessary to make it work.

The organization was entering a new stage of development. Previously, it had operated informally, based on trust. Now the demand was for more formal systems. Recently, over $300,000 in grain was found to be missing from one of the storage facilities. When we arrived to do our analysis, the original CEO had just left his position and the organization was in chaos. The CEO had been unable to manage the organization's transition from a young and informally-driven entity to one based on clearer systems and roles and responsibilities.

work. Successful performance at this stage means continual growth of the organization and the recognition by its stakeholders that it is filling a valuable niche. Poor performance at this stage can mean an early demise. If the organization survives, it still may have to reinvent itself by refocusing what it is doing in order to become firmly established. Throughout this inception period when the organization is struggling to survive and succeed, the patterns of organizational behavior and personality are shaped.

Adolescence

If the young organization is successful and finds resources to support its growth, it enters into its adolescent stage. Growing pains are difficult; the informality associated with success in early stages gives way to more formal rules and procedures. There is a need for increased strategic thinking, and longer range planning and management for the organization to handle its successes. Typically at this stage, there is a need to involve more people in the management of the organization, as sheer growth and development make it difficult for the leader to juggle all of the responsibilities. The organization is often looking at expanding its services and products at the same time. It has tasted success and is feeling that it has a special place on the map of organizations within which it operates.

However, in this adolescent stage, various levels of resistance and conflict emerge as well. Internally, the call for more organization, rules, procedures and structure is met with resistance from those who flourished under the more free-wheeling birth phase. In some organizations, the adolescent stage is short and protracted, while other organizations seem to continually cycle within this phase. More dynamic organizations are continually seeking new niches and areas for growth and development. They explore new ways to serve their clients and stakeholders, and to create and recreate the excitement of their founding and growth. The downside, however, is that creating and recreating an organization is often inefficient, and there is considerable pressure to regularize and standardize practices to gain efficiency.

The organizational paradox is that the standardization, rules and regulations established to improve efficiency often discourage organizational members, thus creating the opposite of what was desired. The ability to navigate through a sea of favorable and unfavorable forces and to manage paradoxes becomes increasingly important at this stage. From the analyst's perspective, we try to understand how well the organization balanced these forces and how this is affecting its performance. Is it on the road to real maturity?

Adult

By the time an organization reaches maturity, it is guided by set patterns of behavior, structure and rules. It often has a particular approach to its organizational role that is firmly embedded or institutionalized. Although this appears to be a stable time in the organization's life cycle, there are certain pitfalls. If the organization becomes overly bureaucratic and rigid, it runs the risk of reducing its ability to respond to the changing needs of its stakeholders. This may lead to its downfall, or to the perception of those both inside and outside of the organization that it is failing to live up to its potential. On the other hand, more flexible organizations often re-engineer and recreate themselves at this stage of maturity. Some organizations constantly reinvent themselves and stay in this stage for a long time.

Decline

The final stage in the organizational life cycle is the decline. We have witnessed this stage in many government organizations, NGOs, and private sector businesses over the past 10 to 15 years. A number of highly dysfunctional personality traits within the organization are often found at this stage. If the organization had a history of early success, there is now an inability to recognize the new realities of poor performance. There seems to be a considerable amount of political infighting, scapegoating, cynicism, and commitment to old strategies. At this stage, you hear all of the reasons "why it won't work." The organization's history is often dotted with a series of innovations, reorganizations and new approaches that were tried but "failed." The organization is unable to bring people together and focus on overcoming their difficulties. Changes are viewed cynically. People are afraid to fail again.

We saw a great deal of this in the 1980s and 1990s in government organizations, both in developed and developing countries. After a long period of growth, the economic recession led to major decreases in the ability of government agencies to obtain the needed funding. New management techniques were introduced at frightening speeds. Government agencies needed to "do more with less." There were new restructuring schemes, changes in work processing and in the use of information technology, and more focus on performance measurement. Many government agencies unable to change became more cynical and continued to decline. Some faded away; others received dwindling amounts of resources and continued to decline. Others adapted, were revitalized, and experienced a rebirth.

Data on History

The history of an organization is often not so easy to find in a particular place. At one level, it resides within the organization's documents and hard data. The charter and early documents give some insight into early organizational thinking. We can determine relatively easily if organizations are growing or declining by looking at staffing, or at the amount of available financial resources. We obtain a picture by looking at the types of programs or projects the organization worked on. From this data, we can infer about the history.

We can also try to obtain oral history. How do people in the organization perceive its evolution? What do they think are the key milestones? How have these milestones affected the organization's direction? Interviews can give insight into leadership and changes. Similarly, they can provide an understanding of how people perceive organizational shifts at certain stages of development.

Assessing History

One aspect of an organizational assessment is to define the organization's evolutionary stage and identify the characteristics associated with this stage. The various aspects of an organization's evolution may give insights into its life cycle position and personality.

Questions: History

- How has leadership evolved? Have there been changes in leadership? Why?
- Have the roles and strategy of the organization changed over time? In what ways?
- Has the organization's resource base changed over time? How?
- Has the organization restructured or reorganized? How often? In what ways?
- What have been the organization's major successes and crises?
- What are the organization's key milestones?
- Have the organization's products or services increased, decreased or changed over time?

VISION AND MISSION

The vision and the mission of an organization emerge from important social, economic, spiritual and political values. They are meant to inspire and promote organizational loyalty. Vision and mission are those parts of an organization that appeal to the heart; that is, they represent the organization's emotional appeal. They motivate people and draw upon staff and stakeholders' hopes and aspirations. In this sense, the vision and mission of an organization provide inspirational motivation.

Clarifying the vision and mission are important in both private and public sector organizations. Private sector organizations often identify the importance of serving their customers, and have created visions and missions to support this theme. In the public sphere, schools, hospitals and even line ministries have begun to see their roles in terms of service to the public, and have developed vision and mission statements that support such ideas.

At issue for many organizations is not only to write but to then live the statements. When vision and mission statements are not lived up to, the result is not to enhance motivation but to foster cynicism. Assessing an organization's motivation primarily involves looking at its mission, since this is more closely linked to what the organization wants to do. However, in examining the mission, the link to the larger vision, as well as more operational components, must also be assessed.

Definition

An organization's vision defines the kind of a world to which it wants to contribute. A children's organization with which we worked indicated that it wanted a world where "children were free from hunger and able to access the health, educational and social services they needed to become happy and productive citizens." It was this vision about children that motivated the staff and led them to devise a more elaborate statement of the future they wanted. Visions lie beyond the scope of any one organization. They represent the hopes and dreams of organizational members. The vision describes the changes in the prevailing economic, political, social or environmental situation that the program hopes to bring about.

Missions, on the other hand, are a step in operationalizing the vision, an organization's raison d'être. *The mission is an expression of how people see the organization operating.* It exists within the context of the vision, and begins the process of operationalizing the vision into more concrete actions. In this context, the mission lays a foundation for future action (Bart, 1997) and guides the organization's choice of strategies and activities. Some of the main reasons for an organization to have a vision and mission expressed in clear statements are to:

- Promote clarity of purpose
- Function as a foundation for making decisions
- Gain commitment for goals
- Foster understanding and support for its goals.

Whereas the vision locates the organization within a cluster of organizations, it is the mission that answers the questions: Why does this organization exist? Whom does it serve? By what means does it serve them? Those responsible for the performance of an organization increasingly recognize the benefits of clearly and simply communicating the direction in which their organization is going. Such descriptions of the organization's future, whom it serves, what it values, and how it defines success can have a powerful impact on the organization's personality.

Dimensions

Typically, organizations are founded when a prime mover identifies a need that is translated into an idea—a vision, and ultimately, a mission—and then into the desired product or service. The prime mover gathers people around to carry out this task. Some organizations are founded by other means, such as when a new agency is created by a government. But even in these cases, the founding of the agency can be traced to a prime mover. The point is that people who come together do not do so randomly. At the start, they share some values associated with the fledgling organization and often see something in it for themselves. Sometimes, not only does the organization indicate the services it wants to provide, but it also conveys a sense of mission. This is the idea of people coming together to do something that is particularly exciting and motivating.

Clearly, as organizations evolve, they need to create and recreate their mission. They need to spur their staff's enthusiasm. Developing and articulating a mission involves two key dimensions. First, the mission can act as a baseline, something against which organizational members and stakeholders can assess the consistency, alignment and focus of their actions and decisions. From a technical perspective, a mission statement identifies the products and services provided: the clients or customers you are trying to serve; where the organization wants to go; and some articulation of organizational values (Calfee, 1993).

Second, the mission must inspire and motivate members to perform and encourage them to behave in ways that will help the organization achieve success. Organizational analysts increasingly suggest that members need to identify with the organizations in which they are working. The mission statement sets out some of the underlying values that define the organization and support the socialization and indoctrination process. Thus, a key dimension of the mission statement is to reinforce the ideology of the organization.

Data on the Mission

Today, mission statements abound in private and public organizations. You see them in the halls and on the walls of offices of NGOs, government agencies and the world's leading corporations. One of the reasons for their popularity is that they are the cornerstones of an organization's strategy and business plan.

Organizations take a wide variety of approaches to expressing their mission. Some describe a detailed vision of the future and write a mission statement that summarizes this vision. Others summarize their mission in a slogan, a motto, or a single statement or phrase. Ideally, the mission is the written expression of the basic goals, characteristics, values and philosophy that shape the organization and give it purpose.

Through this statement, the organization seeks to distinguish itself from others by articulating its scope of activities, its products, services and market, and the significant technologies and approaches it uses to meet its goals. By expressing the organization's ultimate aims— essentially, what it values most—the mission statement should provide members with a sense of shared purpose and direction. The goals enshrined within a mission statement should serve as a foundation for the organization's strategic planning and major activities, and provide a framework for evaluating organizational performance.

Assessing the Mission

Those seeking to diagnose and analyze the mission of an organization often find themselves dealing with multiple realities—those that are written down, and those that are perceived by organization members. One task in an organizational assessment is to determine the degree to which the formal mission statement is understood and internalized by members and stakeholders of the organization; that is, measure the congruence of the perceived and stated missions. In our own diagnoses, we try to understand if and how the mission is shaping the way that organizational members perceive the organization and its work. Do they help create an organizational personality that defines the organization and the motivation of its staff and stakeholders?

Questions: Vision and Mission

- To what extent is there a clear mission that drives staff behavior?
- To what extent is the mission linked to a larger vision?
- Does the mission give members of the organization a sense of purpose and direction?
- Are organizational members satisfied with the mission statement?
- Does the mission recognize the interests of key stakeholders?
- Is the mission aligned with organizational goals and directions?
- Does the mission reflect the key values and beliefs held by organizational members?
- Does the mission promote shared values?
- Does the mission help sharpen the focus of the organization?
- Do people talk and work toward making progress in pursuing the mission?
- Is the mission seen as a living document? Is it updated and renewed periodically? Are key stakeholders (internal and external) involved in giving meaning to the mission?

CULTURE

Definition

While the mission statement formally articulates organizational purpose, it is the organization's culture that gives life to the organization and helps make the realization of its mission possible. The concept of organizational culture has been the focus of much attention, with analysts associating it with superior corporate performance (Peters and Waterman, 1988), increased productivity (Ouchi, 1981), improved morale, and high rates of return on investment. In an interview with the *Harvard Business Review* (Howard, 1990), the president of Levi Strauss stated:

> We have learned that the soft stuff and the hard stuff are becoming increasingly intertwined. A company's values—what it stands for, what its people believe in—are crucial to its competitive success. Indeed, values drive business.

Organizational culture is the collectively accepted meaning that manifests itself in the formal and informal rules of an organization or a sub-group. The culture embodies the collective symbols, myths, visions and heroes of the organization's past and present. For instance, culture finds expression in the collective pride (and even embellishment) of the accomplishments of individuals. Values important to the organization are illustrated through stories about past successes and failures; these form a living history that guides managers and drives members' behavior. Culture involves what you wear, how you address staff, and what is rewarded and punished. It is often not written. When individuals join an organization, in addition to learning about its formal aspects, they spend much of their time being socialized into the less formal aspects of organizational life—namely its culture (Hatch, 1993).

Dimensions

Diagnosing organizational culture helps us understand the relative levels of consistency or inconsistency of "meaning" that exist in an organization. In some ways, culture is like an iceberg; it has both seen and unseen aspects. From an anthropological perspective, culture has material and non-material dimensions. Culture has both physical artifacts—mission statements, policy guides—as well as basic beliefs that direct the thinking, feelings, perceptions and behaviors of the people in the culture. To know why some people are in trouble, are rejected or punished, or are not appreciated by an organization, you need to know the belief system and norms that underlie the organization's behavior. In this context, four dimensions of organizational culture can be identified: artifacts, perspectives, values, and assumptions (Bloor and Dawson, 1994).

Artifacts are the most tangible aspects of an organization's culture. These are the physical aspects of an organization: the type of office, the logo, dress, rituals (Christmas parties), stories, language and so forth. Artifacts are the physical manifestations of the organization's culture.

Perspectives are the ideas that people hold and use to act appropriately. For example, a perspective includes how the organization handles customer complaints or, for that matter, employee complaints. In some organizations, people go to great lengths to help customers obtain the products and services they say they need. In other organizations, customers are ignored.

Values relate to the ideals held by the organization, including concepts of standards, honesty, quality and integrity.

Underlying or basic *assumptions* are "the taken for granted" beliefs of an organization. This refers to what members of the organization feel is appropriate behavior for themselves and others. Since assumptions are considered a given, they are rarely if ever questioned. The set of tacit assumptions helps form the uniqueness of the organizational culture (Denison, 1996).

Data on Culture

Investigating the dimensions of organizational culture can be deceptive. The culture of an organization is not a single unified element. It can evolve, and may be different at different levels of the organization. In addition, every organization has several sub-cultures, some of which take on most aspects of the dominant organizational culture. Others exist as counter-cultures. Bate (1996) argues that it is a myth to think that an organization is a unified entity with a single culture. Rather, he argues that organizations have many cultures, all vying for dominance. In all organizations, there are predominant trends that may or may not be transitory. In essence, Bate and others argue for using cultural analysis as a way to gain insight into the organization. Understanding the cultural dynamic can help those conducting organizational assessments obtain a more complete picture of the organization.

Where do you find data on the organizational culture? In essence, cultural data surrounds the person doing the organizational assessment. It relates to everything from how people treat people to what is posted on the walls. Thus a starting point for finding data on culture is to observe and feel how an organization works and behaves.

However, personal observations and perceptions one feels as a result of spending time with an organization are not the only sources of information. Clearly, the people in the organization have a wide assortment of information on the culture. Unfortunately, employees and managers are not always articulate or completely aware of the dimensions just discussed. In some instances, they might be aware of some aspects of the culture, but the culture inhibits them from expressing their opinions.

In summary, although culture is an important aspect of organizational motivation, obtaining accurate responses to questions about it can be difficult, and it remains an area that people are reticent to explore (see Box).

CULTURE: A PERSONAL ISSUE

At our recent workshops on institutional and organizational assessment, one exercise was a debate over the question: "Should a donor who is considering providing a grant or loan to an organization conduct an organizational culture assessment as part of its normal diagnostic process?"

This could well be called "the great debate" because of the emotions it generated. Some participants argued that it is the organization that has the responsibility to conduct such assessments, and that donors should not get involved. Others argued that without a supportive culture, no amount of donor support will lead to change in the organization, and therefore donors have a responsibility to examine this area.

Many workshop participants fully believed that culture was often the key element behind poor organizational performance. Several asked rhetorically how organizational members could be expected to be motivated if the organization is corrupt, or when employees need to take outside jobs to make ends meet. No amount of training, they argued, will address this fundamental reality.

Few participants accepted the fact that it could be an area where "outsiders" (donors) could or should intervene. For some, this would be viewed as intrusion; for others, it would be seen as not sufficiently results-oriented.

Assessing Culture

Those who study organizational culture argue that it takes time to diagnose and understand the culture(s) of an organization. While dominant themes might be relatively easy to identify, an effective cultural diagnosis requires an exploration of sub-themes, sub-cultures and underlying assumptions that provide more profound diagnostic insights. The concept of organizational culture can provide diagnosticians with a framework for articulating how the culture of an organization contributes to its motivation and, ultimately, to its performance.

Questions: Culture

- What are the key defining artifacts, values and assumptions that move the organization to perform well or poorly? Why?
- Does the organization attempt to learn about its culture?
- Does the culture support the priorities of the organization?
- Do underlying assumptions support the improvement of performance?
- Do most people in the organization identify with the organization's values?
- Is there a positive attitude toward change?
- Are organizational values and assumptions aligned with the organization's actions?
- Is the dominant organizational culture supported by the various sub-cultures?
- Does the dominant culture seem appropriate for the mission?
- Do the organization's stories and symbols support a desirable culture?

INCENTIVES

Definition

Incentive systems are an important part of organizational motivation and are central to helping diagnosticians understand the forces that drive the organization. *Organizational incentives refer to both the reason for staff to join an organization, and the way an organization rewards and punishes its staff.* Incentive systems can encourage or discourage employee and work group behavior (Allcorn, 1995).

Organizations must continually seek ways to keep their employees and work groups engaged in their work, motivated, efficient and productive. An organization's success can depend on its ability to create the conditions and systems (formal and informal) that entice the best people to work there. Also, a good incentive system encourages employees to be productive and creative, fosters loyalty among those who are most productive, and stimulates innovation (Brudney and Condrey, 1993).

Dimensions

What acts as an incentive for people and groups of people in an organization? Although money is a powerful incentive, it is only part of the incentive system within an organization (see Box). In fact, certain types of financial incentives sometimes reinforce behaviors that work against the interests of the organization. For example, financial incentives that promote individual achievement—such as merit pay for individual accomplishments—can work against building highly productive teams of people.

In general, incentives can be broken down into four main categories. The first involves the use of money. Different types of organizations can offer different types of incentives. Because of their ownership and ability to generate profits, private sector firms offer financial incentives that are often not possible in government or not-for-profit organizations. These include incentives such as pay for reaching productivity targets, bonuses for improved levels of profitability, and stock option plans.

In recent years, hundreds of workers (including secretaries and blue collar workers) in the information technology sector have become millionaires through stock option plans—a type of shared ownership used as part of the incentive system. People in these organizations were asked to work for lower than market rates in exchange for owning shares in the company. Workers reaped benefits far beyond their expectations, although they also shared the potential for loss. Sharing in the rewards that may accrue when an organization does well can be a powerful incentive to work hard and be productive.

OTHER INCENTIVES BESIDES MONEY

Researchers in one organization were asked what kind of incentives would increase their motivation. Surprisingly, although money was cited as an important incentive, the researchers also listed the following as factors that would increase their effectiveness and therefore their motivation: access to better research materials, subscriptions to major publications in their field, access to the Internet to "chat" with other researchers on a specific topic, and the opportunity to present research findings in appropriate forums.

However, some studies conducted in the private sector indicate that economic incentives are only part of an incentive system. People also want other types of incentives. They want to be praised for achievement; they want opportunities for advancement and learning; and they want increasing responsibilities to test their range of competencies. Over the longer term, employees want multiple incentives in their work place. So, although economic incentives are important in the private and public sector, more complex, holistic incentive systems also warrant attention.

A second dimension of incentives relates to more intrinsic factors such as values, security and working conditions. Many people have a strong desire to serve, and thus seek employment that has a redeeming social value, such as with NGOs or in public service. There are, as well, many businesses that provide goods and services for the "public good."

Another set of intrinsic incentives relates to the conditions of employment. Some employees want to have security of employment and other noneconomic rewards such as flexible working hours. These conditions provide incentives for productive workers.

For some workers, their identification with the organization and the cause it serves is an incentive. This is most evident in mission-driven organizations, where motivation is often driven by the power of the organizational mission and other non-economic incentives. Many church-based or development oriented not-for-profit organizations have strong mission service orientations.

Universities and research centers are other examples of organizations with service orientations. However, creating effective incentive systems in research centers in developing countries presents a daunting array of paradoxes. First, the staff is often highly professional and has technical skills that could command higher pay in the private sector market. Researchers, however, often prefer environments that value scientific knowledge and the recognition that emerges from peer review. They seek working environments that encourage wide communication and external stimulation, and that give them the right to decide what research should be conducted. The incentive system must reward their professional behavior in ways that compensate for the discrepancy between what they could earn in the private or government sector, and what they receive in the research center.

Whether they are generating new knowledge through research, working with the poor, or helping the sick, people in the not-for-profit sector are motivated by the calling of their organizational work. They believe in the particular nature of their work, and are often willing to give up some economic incentives for this "service." Today, there is a great deal of publicity given to the good work of such organizations. International agencies support these organizations to foster the provision of services to hard-to-reach groups (the poor, rural, other disadvantaged groups). However, these mission-oriented organizations present similar problems to organizational managers with regard to incentives.

Creating incentive systems that support the efficient use of resources and motivate staff is difficult in any type of organization. The challenge is to find the mix of incentives that will motivate employees to engage in productive and efficient behavior. A further challenge is where to provide organizational incentives. For example, in the public sector, formal incentives are often centralized and beyond the control of senior managers of government agencies. Even the most creative senior managers in the public sector have difficulty managing the incentive system of their agency. This rule of the game is changing in some of the more progressive government agencies.[1]

Data on Incentives

How can information be gathered about an organizational incentive system and the motivational needs of employees? One step is to obtain the documents regarding the organization's salary structures and benefits. If possible, these should be examined in relation to the organization's overall industry.

This only provides the tip of the iceberg, however. Incentives are also in the eyes of the individual. Thus, to obtain data on incentives, it is necessary to create ways to ask employees about the state of the incentive systems that exist within the organization. In some cases, this can be done through face-to-face interviews. However, we found that the best way to gather this type of information is through a combination of questionnaire surveys given to all employees and focus groups based on job category. The survey provides the information that can then be probed more deeply during a group interview or focus group.

Assessing Incentive Systems

What does all this mean for analyzing the incentive systems of an organization? First, it is important to understand the organization's underlying incentive structure. In the private sector organization, economic incentives are an important aspect of the struc-

---

[1] See Osborne and Gaebler (1992) for some ideas about how this is occurring in the United States.

ture; in the public sector, the sense of service to the public is often central; and in not-for-profit organizations, understanding the extent to which the mission drives behavior is paramount. When examining the incentive structure, it is important to identify the specific aspects of the system that either support or divert attention from performance. Are the incentive systems providing the right mixture of economic and noneconomic rewards and punishments? Are they sending the right signals to the individuals and groups in the organization? If not, is there anything the organization can do to correct this, or is it beyond the organization's control?

Questions: Incentives

- Does the organization's incentive system encourage or discourage good staff performance?
- Do people feel rewarded for their work?
- Are people adequately compensated?
- Do non-monetary rewards support good organizational behavior?
- Is the incentive system adequately managed?
- Is there an ongoing review of the incentive system?
- Are people treated equitably in the organization?
- Is there consistency between what people are rewarded for and what the organization says it will reward?

CONCLUSIONS

Each organization and the people within it are motivated to behave in ways that are predictable within that organization. But where does this come from? What are the forces that drive performance?

Organizations have different characteristics at different points in their history and may be motivated by different forces. Young organizations, for example, may be more open to change and re-engineering than more mature organizations. The mission of an organization can be a powerful guiding light, but it is important to determine whether the stated mission really moves people, whether it reflects what the people in the organization believe, or both. Organizational culture, a complex and layered system of values and beliefs, is difficult to diagnose (with all its sub-themes, sub-cultures and underlying assumptions), but is a powerful contributor to motivation and, ultimately, to performance. People are motivated to do well by a variety of incentives, the greatest of which is not always monetary.

Every organization is driven by a unique combination of energy that comes from experience, a vision of the future, some sense of shared values, and anticipated rewards. Taken together, these factors constitute organizational motivation. Understanding what motivates an organization can be a powerful tool in assessing and improving its performance.

Chapter Five

PERFORMANCE

The analysis of organizational performance is a crucial step in the organizational assessment process. Yet, measuring performance is one of the most problematic issues in the field of organizational theory (Steers, 1975; Zammuto, 1982; Handa and Adas, 1996). While there are a number of approaches to assessing organizational performance, there is little consensus as to what constitutes a valid set of criteria.

In the 1950s, performance was referred to as the *extent to which an organization as a social system fulfilled its objectives* (Georgopoulos and Tannenbaum, 1957). In the 1960s and 1970s, Yuchtman and Seashore (1967) defined performance as *the ability of an organization to exploit its environment to access scarce resources*. In the 1980s and 1990s, as constructivist thinking became more standard in organizational theory, it was recognized that identifying organizational goals is more complex than first thought. A measurement of organizational performance needs to involve the perceptions of the organization's multiple constituencies or stakeholders, including those who work within the organization (Hassard and Parker, 1993). In other words, the concept of organizational performance is, at least in part, individually constructed. The influence or power of different stakeholders determines which performance message is dominant.

Broadly speaking, the organizational development literature discusses performance at four levels:

- The individual employee (performance appraisal)
- The team or small group (team performance)
- The program (program performance)
- The organization (organizational performance).

In our framework, we reserve the concept of organizational performance for the overall organizational result (the combined results of individual, team and program performance). Every organization has work to do and some way of measuring and communicating how well it does this work. While there are multiple ways of understanding performance, in most sectors and development areas, there are conventional yardsticks that give some direction to understanding that performance.

Education ministries, for example, may measure their performance in terms of their contribution to children's learning. Health ministries may measure in terms of their contribution to the care and treatment of the sick. Energy companies may measure performance in terms of supplying electricity. Municipalities are often compared on the basis of the quality of life available to their citizens, while in the private sector, the conventional measure is profitability, since companies that ignore making a profit risk their survival.

Stakeholders are interested in the ways an organization defines its results and communicates these to its various publics (Blickendorfer and Janey, 1988). Each stakeholder or constituency group has its own interests, as well as a concept of what constitutes good performance. At the program level, beneficiaries have a primary interest in the performance of the program, and a secondary interest in organizational performance. Clearly, employees have an important stake in the performance of the organization upon which they depend for their livelihood. At the level of organizational performance, there are other constituents such as citizens, funders, politicians and investors, all of whom have yet other sets of interests (Boschken, 1994).

DIFFERENT EXPECTATIONS OF PERFORMANCE

The customers of a hydroelectric plant want reliable electrical service, while the government wants to reduce its subsidies to the plant. The government might be willing to accept a lower standard of service if it means lower costs.

In research centers, scholarly researchers might define performance in terms of the number of published articles, whereas senior administrators might define it as the quantity of financial resources brought into the research center through grants.

In both of these situations, you might find still another group of stakeholders (outside investors or donors) who see performance in terms of improved access to hydroelectric power or to the use of research.

In fact, all of these notions of performance may be congruent with the purpose of the organization under review.

In the private sector, for example, people who invest in an organization—an important stakeholder group—are more interested in profitability and return on investment as a performance issue than are the organization's employees or beneficiaries. Each interest group or stakeholder in an organization may have a different concept of what constitutes "good" performance.

Amid all these levels and layers of complexity, what are the elements that should be assessed in analyzing the performance of an organization? In our analyses, we attempt to integrate the various schools of thought and devise a multi-dimensional and comprehensive framework for understanding organizational performance that is useful in analyzing any organization. We believe that organizational performance has four main elements: *effectiveness, efficiency, relevance and financial viability.*

PERFORMANCE IN RELATION TO EFFECTIVENESS

Definition

The starting point for assessing the performance of an organization is its effectiveness. The definition of effectiveness used here is fundamentally embedded in our understanding of the word *organization*. Organizations are commonly defined as instruments of purpose. Using the classical definition of organization (Etzioni, 1964), every organization is set up for a particular function that is clarified through its goals. The goals are made visible through the results of the organization's work and activities in pursuit of these goals.

Within our framework, organizational effectiveness is a prerequisite for the organization to accomplish its goals. Specifically, we define organizational effectiveness as *the extent to which an organization is able to fulfill its goals.* As stated by March and Sutton (1997): "Explaining variation in performance or effectiveness is one of the more enduring themes in the study of organizational performance."

However, describing and measuring effectiveness presents problems. First, it is unclear whether you can decide on a single set of goals or, for that matter, come to consensus about a multiple set of goals for an organization (Brown, 1994). Second, it is unclear where to go, and to whom to go to, to identify goals or seek consensus. Despite these difficulties, organizations do engage in a variety of processes to identify their goals, objectives and systems to communicate their effectiveness—that is, the extent to which they attain their goals—to their constituents.

Dimensions

What are the component parts or the dimensions of effectiveness? What is the experience? In general, there are no common dimensions of effectiveness across all organizations. This is common sense. The goals of a community NGO are not the same as the goals of an environmental NGO; nor are they the same as those of the Ministry of Finance. Nevertheless, despite the variety of organizations that exist, there are great similarities among various functional groupings of organizations (Heckman, Heinrich and Smith, 1997).

Most Ministries of Education are concerned with imparting adequate skills in reading, writing and math. While it might have other dimensions to its mandate, a Ministry of Education would have little reason to exist if it were not responsible for organizing itself to provide basic skills for its society. Thus, Ministries of Education organize themselves to deliver programs that meet these and other goals. Similarly, Ministries of Finance have a functional responsibility for the economic and financial aspects of a nation's business.

In assessing the effectiveness of an organization, it is important to first understand its functional purpose (for example, for a university to provide higher learning), and then to explore the way the organization understands the various dimensions (teaching, research and service) of its function. Sometimes an organization's understanding of its function and dimensions of effectiveness differs from that of its stakeholders. In other cases, the balance the organization places on its dimensions differs among stakeholders. When this happens, stakeholders are dissatisfied, a problem that organizations need to address.

Trying to appreciate the dimensions of organizational effectiveness requires some understanding of the functional purposes of the category of organizations within which the organization fits. These functional purposes give insight into the dimensions of organizational effectiveness.

A review of the university literature finds that, in general, the functional purpose of universities has led to three broad dimensions of university work: teaching, research and service. A similar set of dimensions was identified for research centers, although instead of formal teaching leading to degrees, research centers sometimes provide nondegree-oriented training.

In a different context, we worked with municipalities organized to improve the quality of life of those residing within their jurisdiction. In reviewing their effectiveness, we discovered some 20 dimensions in which the municipalities engage to improve the lives of their citizens. Some of these services address basic human needs, such as the quality of water and sanitation, for which municipalities are responsible. Other services are less basic. In many Canadian provinces, for example, municipalities take on the responsibility of organizing recreational services.

The dimensions of organizational effectiveness are simultaneously stable and dynamic. They are stable from the perspective of the role of the organization in fulfilling the implicit promise that relates to its existence; that is, education is the goal of schools, improved health the goal of hospitals. Although the dimensions vary among the different organizational types, there is some stability within a specific type of organization (Heckman, Heinrich and Smith, 1997).

From another perspective, the dimensions of effectiveness are stable and dynamic because within any type of organization, the importance of a particular indicator of effectiveness varies with respect to the particular stakeholder (Wohlstetter, 1994). For example, in private sector organizations, profitability is commonly one of the organizational goals. However, profitability means different things to different stakeholders. To a worker, it might mean foregone wages with an implicit agreement that a profitable firm leads to long-term employment. To a manager, profit might mean a bigger salary through stock options. To an investor, it might mean better returns on investment.

Assessing Effectiveness

Assessing the effectiveness of not-for-profit and government organizations is no easy task. Given that we define effectiveness as the extent to which an organization is meeting its functional goals, the first order of business in assessing organizational effectiveness is to identify the goals.

As stated, at one level the organizational goals are self-evident: Ministries of Education educate children. From a functional perspective, assessing the effectiveness of an organization requires some understanding of its functional responsibilities. As one becomes more familiar with the organization under review, the purpose and goals are made explicit in various organizational documents—the charter, incorporation documents, or the organizational plan or strategy. In government departments, these are outlined in legislation that sets up the department.

Mission statements provide particularly important insight into the organization's purpose and goals. The U.S. General Accounting Office, for example, requires the plan of its executing agents (organizations) to first identify goals and the measures covering these goals. Once the organization's purpose, goals and dimensions are clear, the diagnostician is ready to embark on the assessment.

The first step is to decide on a set of questions to guide the process of exploring the extent to which the organization is effective. An important aspect in developing questions is to recognize that some questions are broader than others. In fact, questions can go from extremely broad— What is the quality of teaching at the university?—to extremely specific—What percentage of the teachers received excellent in the student rating system? As you move to specificity within the questioning process, you begin to identify the potential indicators that can help answer the question. These indicators allow for measuring the concept under review and give insight into the issue of effectiveness (see Lusthaus et al., 1999, p. 22).

Is One Goal Better than Another?

In a recent review of a health research center, we assessed the charter, as is common practice. It indicated that the center was supposed to engage in research, training and service. As part of the service dimension, the charter stipulated that the center was responsible for running a hospital, among other community services.

Over the 40 or so years of its existence, this research center became quite prestigious and attracted a number of upwardly mobile academics to its staff. For such mobile academics to continue a research career, it is essential that they publish in refereed journals.

On the other hand, all the documents of the research center, as well as statements by the center director, indicated that the "ultimate aim" of the center was to translate research into policy and practice. In other words, the basis for judging success was not simply academic work, but rather, the use of the research—whether it made it into refereed journals or not. The center offered a significant amount of detail on publications by center staff, but there was relatively little systematically gathered information on the use of that research for either policy or practice.

Assessing the effectiveness of an organization is more elusive than it appears. For example, organizations sometimes emphasize one of the goals at the expense of others. Is the research center described in the accompanying box effective if it publishes a significant number of refereed journals? What can be used to indicate that a research center is effective? Or for that manner, when can it be stated that a Ministry of Education or Finance is effective? These are quite perplexing questions that make the assessment of effectiveness very difficult.

Questions: Effectiveness

- *How effective is the organization in moving toward the fulfillment of its mission?*
- *How effective is the organization in meeting those goals as expressed in its charter, mission statement or other documents that provide the "raison d'être" for the organization?*
- *Is the mission operationalized through program goals, objectives and activities?*
- *Are quantitative and qualitative indicators used to capture the essence of the mission?*
- *Is there a system for assessing effectiveness, that is, the extent to which goals and objectives are realized?*
- *Do customers or beneficiaries for whom a line of business or program is designed judge it to be satisfactory?*
- *Does the organization monitor organizational effectiveness?*
- *Does the organization use feedback to improve itself?*

Indicators of Effectiveness

Does your organization have indicators of effectiveness? If not, now is the time to develop some preliminary indicators to guide your assessment and begin a process to help the organization develop indicators and collect data on effectiveness for the future (*Healthcare Financial Management*, 1997). Questions need answers, and those answers come from various sources of data, including people, documents and analysis. But how do you move from a question to data sources?

Some people find it helpful to identify indicators that help answer the questions. Clearly, a first step in this search is to identify the indicators the organization uses (if any) to describe its effectiveness or proxies of these indictors (i.e., the extent to which the organization contributes to some higher order indicator). Since each organization type—be it a municipality or an NGO—varies in its function, purpose, goals and dimensions, the indicators of effectiveness similarly vary (Tavenas, 1992).

One difficulty in assessing organizational effectiveness occurs when the organization has not created a set of indicators. Under these conditions, it is necessary to develop, with the organization, a proxy list of indicators, and to collect data on effectiveness. As is the case with the questions associated with effectiveness, there is no set list of indicators usable for all organizations (Eimicke, 1998). Below, however, are what might be called "indicator starting points" that can be used when an organization does not have its own set of indicators:

- Achievement of goals
- Number of clients served
- Quality of services/products
- Service access and usage
- Knowledge generation and utilization
- Quality of life changes
- Demand for services or products
- Replication of the organization's programs by stakeholders
- Growth indicators for coverage of programs, services, clients and funding.

PERFORMANCE IN RELATION TO EFFICIENCY

Definition

The second general concept for judging organizational performance is efficiency. Every organization has a certain level of resources to provide goods and services, and must operate within its resource constraints. When an organization's results are measured in relationship to its resources, the measurement yardstick is efficiency. More specifically, we define efficiency as *a ratio that reflects a comparison of outputs accomplished to the costs incurred for accomplishing these goals.*

There are two aspects of efficiency. The first is the units of production or services that relate to the organizational purpose, and the second is how much it costs to produce those goods and services. How wasteful or economical was the organization in producing the outcomes? This is the question of efficiency (Barker, 1995).

Efficiency is generally measured as the ratio of outputs to inputs. This implies that to attain efficiency, an organization must ensure that maximum outputs are obtained from the resources it devotes to a program, operation or department (Tavenas, 1992). Conversely, efficiency is achieved when the minimum level of resources is used to produce the target output or to achieve the objectives of a program, operation or department.

In today's competitive economies, organizations must provide exceptional products and services within an appropriate cost structure. In times of economic constraint, performance is increasingly judged by the efficiency of the organization (the cost per service, the number of outputs per staff, publications per employee) (Barker, 1995). By using the monetary values or costs and benefits that are inevitably part of efficiency, it is possible to determine on a quantitative basis where to invest in programs (better value for money), what products and services are becoming obsolete, and which activities are not providing adequate value for the money. Whatever the overall size of the unit, organizations viewed as performing well are those that provide good value for the money expended.

Dimensions

Around the world, organizations face increasing pressure to use their resources wisely. Globalization generally involves lower taxes and rising costs of human and natural resources, all of which combine to push an efficiency agenda in most organizations. Over the last decade, both private and public organizations have been forced to reduce costs and increase productivity through downsizing or rightsizing exercises. "Do more with less" is the rallying cry for many organizations in both the developed and the developing world. In other words, produce more results with less resources (Eimicke, 1998).

In the private sector, particularly in manufacturing, tremendous gains have been made by re-engineering production to improve efficiency. Information technology, along with other technologies, dramatically improved productivity. However, as you move from manufacturing systems to more people-oriented and politically controlled systems, the issues of efficiency are more difficult to understand (Heckman et al., 1997).

First, in politically dominated systems, efficiency (costs in relation to the accomplishment of goals) is often complicated because unstated goals are as important, if not more important, than stated goals. For example, in many countries, government operated or regulated railroad companies are used to employ people who are loyal or supportive to the government, regardless of their productivity. In other instances, many not-for-profit organizations value human relationships above efficiency measures, though this is often not stated.

In general, there are two approaches to describing organizational efficiency, although neither is well developed for either government or not-for-profit organizations. The first approach is the more standard definition of efficiency. It tries to link the quantity of resources used to the results obtained. Historically, this type of indicator provides a broad view of an organization and allows for comparisons across organizations.

While this approach has met with some success, there is another way to describe the extent to which an organization is "administratively efficient." Administrative efficiency explores how different work processes contribute to the overall value added in an organization. Simons and Davila (1999) call this the return on management—a measure of how well an organization is managing its strategy and work processes.

Unlike historical methods of efficiency that lead to more precise percentages of return, this measure of efficiency provides a rough estimate of the amount of productive energy expended by an organization in relation to the amount of managerial and professional time invested. In other words, it measures how well the systems produced by managers and other professionals facilitate the productive energy of the organization.

This dimension is linked to the ability of an organization to balance policies, procedures and creative efforts by addressing roles and responsibilities that either help or stifle staff, or the fact that there are either too many or not enough rules. In sum, this second approach to measuring efficiency assesses the extent to which organizational strategy, systems and procedures generate productive energy.

Assessing Efficiency

In assessing efficiency, it is generally more difficult to assess outputs than inputs, especially in service organizations, where outputs tend to be qualitative rather than quantitative.[1] Even in organizations that produce tangible physical products, it still may be difficult to obtain a timely and ideal assessment of output that captures quality differences over time or across firms (Bowles and Coates, 1993).

For example, if the efficiency of a research organization is measured in terms of the number of research papers written per researcher, the question of the quality of those papers is overlooked. To capture this quality consideration in an efficiency indicator, output can be measured in terms of the number of research articles published in reputable or refereed journals. Those outputs can then be related to the costs of the producers. This example underscores the need for care in deciding on the best choice of indicator that gives a quantitative measure of efficiency but also captures some aspects of product or service quality. In some government ministries,

---

MEASURING EFFICIENCY OUTPUTS

In early 1998, we assessed the efficiency of a subunit of an organization that provided study tours for senior municipal government officials in China. The study tours were held in Canada. The organization was criticized for spending too much money on the tour and not paying enough attention to critiques that a number of people on the tour were not interested in learning about Canadian municipalities. *What are the issues with respect to organizational efficiency?*

We were interested in the criticism and the basis for it. Were there concerns about the overall unit cost per participant day, a characteristic of efficiency? Were there concerns about the administrative costs per participant?

Most of the criticism related not only to the study tour and its costs, but rather to its results—specifically, the benefits of the organization's work to Canada and China. We undertook to find out the costs and benefits of the study tour to Canada, but we found that the organization did not collect data on the benefits. We therefore created our own benefits database and designed a system to evaluate overall efficiency with respect to results.

We devoted several months to the assignment and tapped into the expertise of a wide assortment of Chinese and Canadian participants, as well as other people involved with the tours. The results were a model combining concrete historical performance with forecasting of benefits. Much to the amazement of the critics, when the results were in, Canada obtained $18 worth of benefits for every dollar it put into the organization. Is this efficient? We said yes, but suggested that it was necessary to obtain some comparisons in the future.

---

[1] We often use outputs as a proxy because of the difficulty of measuring outcomes and the costs of outputs.

qualitative indicators are the most important. For example, how do you assess the efficiency of foreign ministries? Is it the cost of the ministry in relation to the quality of its international relationships? The country image?

Questions: Efficiency

- What is the relationship between the unit of output and the cost of producing the outcome?
- How efficiently is the organization using its human, financial and physical resources?
- Are costs of staff members related to their productivity?
- Are physical facilities (buildings, equipment, etc.) used optimally?
- Are financial resources used optimally? What are the comparative ratios of costs and results?
- Are there administrative systems in place that provide good value for costs?
- Are there quality administrative systems in place to support efficiency (financial, human resources, program, strategy, etc.)?
- Does the organization make benchmarked comparisons based on the performance of similar programs, or on the performance of the program itself over time, or on some predetermined target at the beginning of the program?

Indicators of Efficiency

As with effectiveness, if an organization has not developed efficiency indicators, there are some preliminary indicators that can be used to guide an assessment:

- Cost per service or program provided
- Overhead to total service or program cost
- Outputs per staff
- Cost per client served
- Employee absenteeism and turnover rates
- Program completion rates
- Frequency of system breakdowns
- Timeliness of delivery of services.

Efficiency and effectiveness are traditional concepts used by organizational practitioners to evaluate performance. An organization is efficient if, compared with similar organizations, its results are relatively high in relation to the resources expended. It is effective to the extent that it reaches its intended purpose or goals. However, organizations can be highly effective without being efficient, and can reach relatively high levels of efficiency without being effective (March and Sutton, 1997).

Effectiveness and efficiency, however, do not tell the whole story of organizational performance. Today, organizations must be, and must be seen as, continually relevant to their stakeholders. Ongoing relevance is the third concept of performance.

PERFORMANCE IN RELATION TO ONGOING RELEVANCE

Definition

In modern organizational literature, organizations are portrayed as webs of relationships among stakeholders (Weick, 1995). These groups vie for importance and power within the organization and try to influence the choice of criteria the organization uses for determining performance. From a stakeholder perspective, the performance of an organization is understood as the extent to which the needs and requirements of each stakeholder are met. Organizations must be relevant to their key stakeholders. In studying development NGOs, we find the requirements and expectations of their donors are not the same as the requirements of their clients (another stakeholder group). These organizations need to be relevant to both funders and clients, and must reconcile the differences.

Organizations in any society take time to evolve and develop, but over time they must create ways to renew themselves in order to remain useful to their major stakeholders. While all organizations ultimately face internal and external crises, the survivors are those that succeed in adapting to changing contexts. From a system perspective, for an organization to survive, it must obtain support from its environment. In other words, an organization must supply stakeholders in the environment with the goods and services they want, need and are willing to support. A key performance variable is the ongoing relevance of an organization, which we define as *the ability of an organization to meet the needs and gain the support of its priority stakeholders in the past, present and future.*

In the private sector, the organizational literature captures the notion of relevance through innovation and adaptation. To emerge as a "learning organization," an organization must strive for the ideal of constantly adapting to the changing environment and to the evolving needs of its stakeholders. Peter Senge argues that organizations that survive are those that learn on a continuous basis and use the learning acquired to improve and perform (Senge et al., 1994, 1999).

In today's context, organizational performance relates to the ability of the organization to keep its mission, goals, programs and activities aligned with the evolving needs of its key stakeholders and constituents. In most of the literature on the private, public administration and development sectors, clients and customers are identified as central stakeholders in assessing the performance of an organization. However, most organizations have a range of stakeholders whose support is essential if the organization is to remain relevant. Organizations must set priorities and accordingly address the conflicts and paradoxes among their stakeholder groups.

Which stakeholder should be satisfied? How should these sets of expectations be managed? In a health care facility, we found that being relevant to the government by cutting costs and services led to being less client-oriented (meeting needs of patients and their families). In the development context, doing more for less

THE STRUGGLE FOR RELEVANCE

A research center in Eastern Africa was perceived as successful because it obtained funding and funding renewals from donor agencies; its researchers wrote papers published in good journals; and it was efficient in conducting research. Yet, as the center began to assess its ongoing relevance to its stakeholders, two conflicting sets of expectations emerged. One of the center's most important stakeholders was a funding agency that supported the development of policy research. To meet the needs of this stakeholder, the research center devoted considerable resources to policy research. It created a policy research unit and recruited staff with appropriate expertise in this area. But another important stakeholder of the center was the local civil society, which did not view policy research as useful for the community, expecting instead that the research center focus more resources on applied research.

might be a useful slogan for donors and their taxpayers, but not necessarily satisfying for development workers who are already putting in 60 hour weeks and are away from home a third of the time.

Dimensions

Ongoing relevance is central to the long-term viability of any organization. In the private sector, relevance is dramatically linked to the reaction of the market to the goods, services and information the organization provides to the market. Nowhere is this seen more dramatically and directly than in the way the present stock market responds to information about a company.

When new products or innovations are announced, or when profits from the quarter are made public, market investors make immediate judgments on the ongoing relevance of the firm to its major stakeholders (customers, investors, staff, suppliers, etc.). A judgment is made about the future of the organization. Government and not-for-profit organizations rarely receive this type of immediate feedback about their relevance and thus need to rely on different types of feedback.

We use two basic dimensions for assessing ongoing organizational relevance. The first relates to *the ability of an organization to keep its key stakeholders satisfied*. To perform well, the organization must make the key stakeholders feel that their expectations are being met. In government and not-for-profit organizations, one way to determine this is to seek information on the perceptions of satisfaction of the stakeholders (taxpayers, clients, staff, suppliers, etc.)

However, this dimension is quite limiting and sometimes paradoxical. As illustrated in the box on the East African research center, different stakeholders hold contradictory expectations (cut health care costs, increase client satisfaction). What this calls for is the second dimension of ongoing relevance, which is *the ability to innovate and create new and more effective situations as a result of insight and new knowledge*. Innovation and adaptation to changing requirements are crucial performance indicators in today's fast-paced world.

Assessing Relevance

Organizations need to develop ways to understand the perceptions of their key stakeholders, and over the past decade, organizations significantly increased expenditures to do just that. Today, private firms spend increasing amounts to assess consumer reactions to new products and services. Along the same lines, private firms recognize the importance of government as a stakeholder in their businesses and invest heavily in developing associations and lobby groups that both help them understand and influence this stakeholder group.

Similarly, government and not-for-profit organizations have recognized the importance of being relevant. Both groups now systematically assess the quality of their client—"customer" service. Increasingly, these organizations also turn to polling to find out more about the needs and wants of their stakeholders. Do citizens think they are obtaining adequate services for their tax dollars? Are government clients obtaining adequate services from service providers? When stakeholders feel their needs are not met, they may act against the organization's interests through protests or by withholding funds.

Issues related to keeping multiple constituencies satisfied range from maintaining the reputation of the organization in the wider community, to the effects of the organization's programs and services on its beneficiaries or clients, and the effects of management on staff morale.

While part of ongoing relevance is simply meeting stakeholder expectations, another factor is anticipating their needs. Innovation and adaptation to changing conditions are other aspects of ongoing relevance, albeit more speculative ones. Organizations need to anticipate the future, create new products and services, and

---

Questions: Relevance

- Are clients adequately surveyed or polled to obtain their perceptions of the organization?
- Has the organization adapted and changed its work over time?
- Are programs reviewed and revised regularly to reflect a changing environment and capacities?
- Is the mission of the organization reviewed on a regular basis?
- Are assessments of stakeholder needs conducted regularly?
- Does the organization regularly review the environment in order to adapt its strategy accordingly?
- Does the organization monitor its reputation?
- Does the organization create or adapt to new technologies?
- Does the organization encourage innovation?

engage their stakeholders with respect to their emerging needs. At one level, this is seen in every new budget brought down by government. New programs are introduced and old programs disappear. It is often said that a government department is outdated when it does not adequately engage in trying to improve upon its products and services, or when its staff is no longer motivated to try innovative ideas. Trying to assess innovativeness and adaptability are important parts of ongoing relevance.

Indicators of Relevance

Since many organizations do not take into account relevance indicators, it may be necessary to develop some preliminary indicators, such as the following, to guide an assessment:

- Stakeholder satisfaction (clients, international financial institutions, donors, etc.)
- Number of new programs and services
- Changes in partner attitudes
- Role changes
- Changes in funders (quality and quantity)
- Changes in reputation among peer organizations
- Acceptance of programs and services by stakeholders
- Support earmarked for professional development
- Number of old and new financial contributors (risk of discontinuance, leverage of funding)
- Changes in organizational innovation and adaptability (changes appropriate to needs, methods)
- Changes in organizational reputation among key stakeholders
- Changes in services and programs related to changing client systems.

PERFORMANCE IN RELATION TO FINANCIAL VIABILITY

Definition

Organizations can be relatively effective, efficient and relevant to most of their stakeholders, yet on the verge of collapse. How can this be? Over the past three years, our work with government and not-for-profit organizations made us realize that to perform well, an organization must also pay attention to its ability to generate the resources it requires. This means not only having the ability to pay its operational bills, but also having some excess of revenues over expenses (profit or surplus) (Booth, 1996). Whether in the private sector, where profits are a measure of financial health, or in public sectors that rely on funding or loans from government or development banks, financial viability is a key short- and long-term concern.

We have added financial viability as a performance criterion since our 1995 volume. This is because of the large number of not-for-profit and government organizations that today are required to be more market driven. They must focus more attention on the demand and revenue side of their work rather than just the supply side (Henke, 1992). This concept is easily grasped in the private sector, but less so by organizations supported by taxpayers. By financial viability, we mean *the ability of an organization to raise the funds required to meet its functional requirements in the short, medium and long term.*

Dimensions

There are three dimensions to assessing the financial viability of an organization. The first relates to *the ability of an organization to generate enough cash to pay its bills, and in the case of not-for-profit organizations, to be prosperous and profitable.* The concern here is with both short- and long-term cash flow requirements. Resources are generated through an organization's ability to create, supply and deliver products, services or programs useful to customers, clients or beneficiaries (Henke, 1992). When there is a direct purchase of services, customers buy products or services and pay for the services. Donors and governments act as third parties in purchasing products and services they believe are needed or wanted by beneficiaries. Customers and government donors provide the resources an organization needs to survive in the short, medium, and long term. In the short term, an organization needs cash to pay its immediate obligations (payroll, supplies, rent).

Organizations unable to meet their short-term obligations present a risk to their creditors, those to whom they provide services, and people working in the organization (Lampe and Sutton, 1997). This is seen in several ways. In some countries governments pass budgets, but do not provide the cash identified in the budget. As such, the government staff and clients are always feeling betrayed by broken promises.

Organizations also need to generate resources for mid- and long-term obligations. In government agencies, this is not viewed as an issue, because all government capital expenses are expensed the year of purchase. However, with the rapidi-

FINANCIAL VIABILITY: DEALING WITH CHANGE

In 1996, we worked with a community NGO in South Africa that provided educational support services to poor schools in rural districts. From 1985 until 1995, the NGO had received direct support from international agencies whose motive was to fight the South African apartheid regime. In the mid-1990s, it became clear that when an elected government emerged in South Africa, this type of donor support for NGOs would change. Instead of providing direct support to NGOs, donors would give aid funds to the legitimate government, which in turn would distribute the funds.

In other words, it was clear several years before independence that the funding system for the NGO community would change, and that organizations such as the one we assessed would be vulnerable to this change. Our assessment for one of the NGO's funders showed the organization had done outstanding work. It provided first-rate teacher education for poor schools at modest costs. Teachers, administrators and parents were all enthusiastic about the program. Nevertheless, because the NGO had been unable to anticipate the change in funding patterns and find new funding sources, it closed in 1997.

ty of technological change, governments as well as not-for-profit organizations will need to have clear financial plans and methods for implementation allowing for capital replacement.

The second dimension of assessing financial viability deals with *the sources and types of revenues on which the organization bases its costs.* Traditionally, in government agencies, the source of revenue is anticipated taxes. Poorer countries and government departments also rely on various donors to provide funds for their work. The concern addressed by this dimension is the reliability of the flow of funds. With not-for-profit organizations, we analyzed the diversity and reliability of the different funding sources. Organizations that rely on a single funding source without a legal (contractual) or moral funding obligation encounter more difficulty than organizations with multiple, reliable funding sources.

The third dimension is *the ability of an organization to live within its allocation.* Is the organization able to manage within its revenue sources without creating a deficit? This dimension focuses on the actual ability to manage a budgeting process, as well as the results of the process. Financial viability depends on good financial management practices. This is true for both private and public sector organizations. The fact that organizations sell on credit means that it is possible to make profits on paper and still run out of cash, at least in the short term. An NGO can have many contracts signed, but not enough funds to pay bills.

Therefore, short-term financial viability is influenced to a large extent by how effectively the organization manages cash, accounts receivable, and accounts payable. Although there is a perception that financial management requirements are less stringent in the not-for-profit sector, organizations in this sector must nonetheless manage their resources well enough to convince donors and other stakeholders to supply additional funds in the future.

In a general sense, an organization is financially viable if it generates enough value (both internally and from external sources) to keep stakeholders committed to the organization's continued existence. In the case of many public and not-for-profit organizations (NGOs, foundations), staying financially viable depends crucially on management's ability to maintain existing linkages or create new ones to ensure a continued flow of funds over time from diverse sources.

Assessing Financial Viability

Assessing an organization's financial position is an increasingly important aspect of evaluating the organization's overall performance. In simple terms, to survive, an organization must generate at least the amount of resources that it expends. In systems terms, this is homeostasis. However, an organization must constantly draw

---

Questions: Financial Viability

- Is the organization able to generate revenues to respond to the needs of its stakeholders?
- Is the organization creating profits (for-profit groups) or surplus (not-for-profit groups)?
- Is there continued and sustained support from existing funding sources?
- Does the organization consistently obtain new funding sources?
- Does the organization depend on a single source of funding?
- Does the organization consistently have more revenue than expenses?
- Can the organization sustain itself within a competitive environment?
- Are assets greater than liabilities?
- Does the organization keep a reasonable surplus of money to use during difficult times?
- Does the organization monitor its finances on a regular basis?
- Does the organization monitor capital assets and depreciation?

KEY PUBLIC SECTOR FUNCTIONS FOR TRANSITION TO A MARKET ECONOMY

Arturo Israel (1990) of the World Bank has highlighted four positive public sector functions that are crucial for the transition to a market-driven, private sector economy.

The first function is the capacity to design, monitor and implement a consistent set of macroeconomic and sectoral policies. As market and financial liberalization progresses, this function becomes more important as governments lose the capacity to mask and stretch out the costs of fiscal indiscipline, inappropriate exchange rate management, and monetary expansion. According to Israel, if this capacity is not in place, nothing else will work very well. In Africa, for example, strengthening macroeconomic policy analysis has generally not been effectively linked to strengthening policy reform implementation and management, especially for fiscal and budgetary policy.

The second function is the capacity to provide an enabling context for private and public sector activities to operate in competitive environments. This involves three main sub-categories. The first involves dismantling the disabling environment by modifying or eliminating the functions of state agencies that controlled and dominated the private sector. Key areas here are customs, foreign exchange controls, industrial licensing and financial controls. The second is effectively maintaining a level playing field by regulating non-competitive markets and enforcing financial and technical standards. The third is promoting key sectors such as export promotion or domestic food production.

The third function is the capacity to privatize wisely and effectively. Privatization has been too narrowly focused on divestiture. Governments must develop a broader range of options that reflect the reality of very slim markets and high political costs. This involves preparing a strategic plan, and having the capacity to prepare the units for sale or leasing, ensure the fairness and transparency of transactions, and conduct a public awareness campaign to manage the inevitable political tensions that privatization entails. Finally, governments must more effectively operate the enterprises that will remain in the public sector.

The fourth function is the capacity to conduct an effective dialogue with the private sector. In Africa, even those technocrats who have been at the forefront of economic reform efforts have tended to look skeptically at the private sector. Even worse, key public sector agencies that interact with the private sector have looked at business people with a view to controlling them, rather than looking at them as clients with needs and preferences, and with a voice that must be taken into account.

resources from its environment or else it withers. Assessing the financial health of an organization is thus critical to any organizational assessment.

Clearly, the starting point for such an assessment is to review the organization's financial statements. This is a simple procedure for private and not-for-profit sector organizations that involves reviewing income and expense statements over several years, together with the balance sheet and cash flow statements. These documents generally provide most of the information required. In assessing financial viability, lists of accounts receivable and actual contracts should also be requested. Both give insight into the future diversity of funding sources and cash flow schedules.

Ministries view financial viability as less important. Historically, government organizations have not attempted to generate resources or create revenue-producing opportunities. Ministries spend taxpayers' money and other funds (e.g., from donors) to provide services. They are supply-side service providers, and do not have responsibility for either creating demand, or for generating funds to meet the supply needs. However, this concept of government organizations has recently been changing (Osborne and Gaebler, 1992). Increasingly, public policy theorists and practitioners are developing approaches that would make government agencies more sensitive to market forces (Israel, 1990).

By placing government services within market contexts, theorists claim that strong, more viable organizational systems emerge and weaker, poor performing and inefficient organizations disappear.

Indicators of Financial Viability

If the organization does not have financial indicators, it may be necessary to develop some preliminary indicators such as those that follow to guide an assessment.

- Changes over three years to net operating capital
- Ratio of largest funder to overall revenues
- Ratio of cash to deferred revenues
- Ratio of current assets to current liabilities
- Ratio of total assets to total liabilities
- Growth indicators in terms of number of funders, amount of resources mobilized, assets, capital, revenues
- Level of diversification of funding sources
- Frequency or regularity of hiring to provide services.

BALANCING THE ELEMENTS OF PERFORMANCE

In summary, the traditional ideas surrounding organizational performance were limited to the concepts of effectiveness and efficiency—that is, that the organization must meet its goals within an acceptable outlay of resources. However, continued study of organizations increasingly suggests that their performance also incorporates the way they relate and remain relevant to their stakeholders, as well as their ability to attract resources for both the short and long term. To ensure its performance over extended periods of time, the organization must develop and implement appropriate strategies, and its activities and services must remain realistic and connected to stakeholder needs. When an organization's endeavors are not relevant or are too far-reaching and costly, organizational survival is at risk.

In recent years, there has been a great deal more acceptance of the multidimensional aspects of performance. In the United States, government departments are given report cards on about a dozen performance factors. As part of its Government Performance Project, the *Magazine of States and Localities* rates cities on five dimensions. Finally, an increasing number of organizations are aware of the four dimensions of the "balance scorecard" devised by Kaplan and Norton (1996). Balancing the dimensions of performance is becoming more important to understand and to do.

This chapter identified four key elements of organizational performance: *effectiveness, efficiency, relevance and financial viability*. Others categorize the elements of performance with slightly different labels. But regardless of the terminology, it is apparent that all types of organizations struggle to balance the various elements of their performance, and they often need to make strategic tradeoffs between these elements.

Hospital managers, for example, may need to trade off patient care (effectiveness) with the costs that are required to treat patients (efficiency). Tax departments need to trade off ensuring citizen compliance with tax laws (effectiveness) with the need to ensure that citizens believe that the tax department itself is fair (relevance). NGOs must balance the desire to serve people in need (effectiveness) with the need to obtain the funds to pay for the services they provide (financial viability).

At various stages in the life of an organization, its leaders must decide which tradeoffs to make among the elements of performance. The key is to make informed, conscious decisions on these tradeoffs (Kaplan and Norton, 1996).

From the perspective of our organizational assessment framework, the aim is to determine whether the organization and its leaders have good data about organizational performance, and whether they are consciously trying to understand the required performance tradeoffs. Good data and good processes for making those tradeoffs provides a level of confidence in the leadership of the organization.

Chapter Six

METHODOLOGICAL ISSUES IN ORGANIZATIONAL ASSESSMENT

This chapter explores key issues in conducting organizational assessments that respond to the important agendas brought forward by consumers and users. While the chapter provides some general principles and advice for carrying out organizational assessment, it is not intended as a "how to" manual. Rather, the aim is to help the reader understand the considerations needed for effective organizational assessment. An example of an organizational assessment outline is found in Appendix 2.

SOME KEY ISSUES

- Being clear on why people are asking for an organizational assessment
- Understanding the need as analysis or evaluation
- Getting the right questions
- Deciding who will be directly involved in the assessment process
- Understanding the strengths and weaknesses of self-assessment
- Managing the organizational assessment process
- Using suitable data
- Reporting effectively
- Making the organizational assessment process valid

RATIONALE: WHY DO IT?

Before considering how to approach an organizational assessment, you need to reflect on why and for whom it is being done. Assessments typically are initiated by some sponsor, investor or member of an organization, or by the organization itself.

TYPICAL REASONS WHY DIFFERENT STAKEHOLDERS INITIATE AN ORGANIZATIONAL ASSESSMENT

INITIATOR	MAJOR RATIONALE	ORGANIZATIONAL ASSESSMENT FOCUS
Leaders within the organization	■ To celebrate exemplary performance ■ To improve decision making and provide a basis for future strategy development	■ To generate data on four dimensions of performance and determine strengths, weaknesses, opportunities and threats as part of a strategic planning exercise
Board of Directors	■ To exercise their accountability ■ To make key investment decisions. ■ To feed a strategic planning process designed to improve organizational performance	■ To assess performance in its four dimensions ■ To understand how performance could be enhanced ■ To inform the members and guide their role as an investor ■ To guide organizational change by providing a deeper understanding of all aspects of the environment, capability, motivation and performance
External investor	■ To plan the organizational investment strategy so the purpose is achieved ■ To monitor or evaluate an organizational investment to see if it is achieving its intended results	■ To understand the capability deficiencies impeding performance ■ To understand the investment assumptions and risks related to the organization's environment ■ To understand whether there is sufficient motivation within the organization to justify investment ■ To judge whether performance improved as a result of the investment ■ To judge whether the investments in capabilities were implemented as planned ■ To review the design assumptions, including changes in the environment

Some of the main reasons to initiate the assessment are summarized in the accompanying table. Clearly, whoever initiates the assessment shapes the focus. Thus, the agenda is rarely neutral, reflecting instead the needs, interests, values, and preconceptions of the people initiating it. Understanding the overall motivation for initiating an assessment goes a long way toward avoiding problems when implementing it later on.

Given that underdevelopment is to a large extent the result of a constraining institutional framework and non-performing organizations, the ultimate challenge of conducting an organizational assessment and implementing its results is to determine how the intervention can improve the organization's performance.

THE ASSESSMENT PROCESS

Managing an assessment begins with understanding the motivation for conducting it. It is important to know whether the assessment is motivated from within or outside an organization. Those engaged in the assessment need to determine four points: 1) the central purpose of the assessment; 2) the time and budget; 3) the overall approach; and 4) how to communicate and use the information. These matters are ideally contained in written terms of reference that help clarify and communicate the intentions. The form of those terms will vary for an external assessment versus a self-assessment, but in either case, they are useful in keeping the process and vision of the product on track.

Many assessments suffer from poorly prepared terms of reference that are little more than a compilation of questions from various stakeholders. Such terms of reference reflect inexperience and need to be re-cast before a productive assessment can begin. This can be accomplished by better conceptualizing the work plan that responds to the terms of reference. The process of developing these terms can be a major step forward in any organizational assessment, particularly if the process reflects the engagement of stakeholders and clarification of values, issues and other concerns. Indeed, divergent views on the terms of reference are generally an early sign that stakeholders have fundamental differences in perspectives that will not get any easier later in the assessment process.

An overall management structure for the organizational assessment is the human side of what underlies the terms of reference, and as such, needs careful consideration. For external assessments in developed countries, a stakeholder steering committee generally guides the assessment process. Steering committees, however, are not a panacea for successful management. They need to have a defined function beyond just receiving the assessment report. The greatest value of these committees can be to clarify stakeholder interests, values and perspectives on the questions, methodologies and sources of data; engage in vetting of the preliminary findings; address political or other problems; and provide a dynamic forum for debate and challenge of the preliminary draft report. As a management mechanism, steering committees must include the key stakeholders; otherwise there is a risk of imperfect management.

The client-reviewer relationship is generally contractual when the head reviewer is external, though it is often an informal relationship for internal assessment. Formality is advantageous in protecting all interests and in preventing the assessment from becoming the tail that wagged the dog. The contract clarifies the effort and cost involved. Both the terms of reference and the contract formalize the relationship, helping to avoid complications that are all too common, given the political nature of all evaluation work.

What should an assessment cost? This is a question that is always asked by clients. The answer is similar to the response given if asked the cost of building the client a house: it depends on what you want. This is not to advocate an unlimited budget—as the architect will attest, this may be more daunting than to have a circumscribed budget. It is possible to do a quick assessment in a week, at minimal cost; on the other hand, it can involve many months and consume hundreds of thousands of dollars. Assessments vary in scope, and organizations vary in their complexity.

How long should an assessment take? Because of the complexity, it is not possible to do a thorough assessment quickly. A rapid assessment that takes a few days can, however, provide an overall impressionistic view and examine certain aspects. A valid and complete assessment takes three to six months; any longer than that and it risks the difficulty of trying to hit a moving target. The assessment needs to be sufficiently concentrated both to provide for the logistics in a cost-effective way and to convey the seriousness of the endeavor. On the other hand, the time span needs to be long enough to address the core issues fairly. An assessment intended for a major loan for an organization needs to be more robust than one intended to give the new director a sense of the major challenges ahead.

An effective assessment team requires division of labor and coordination mechanisms. Specified roles and areas of responsibility linked to an overall work plan avoid many problems. The team needs to meet for coordination purposes, and it is also helpful to have a continual exchange of such data as interview transcripts, key tables and graphs, and a running list of tentative findings. Every team requires a competent leader skilled at project and process management.

GUIDING THE ASSESSMENT: CHOOSING QUESTIONS

The framework described in previous chapters provides a comprehensive approach to organizational assessment. In reality, however, the assessment is tailored to the needs perceived by the stakeholders who initiate it. Whether in-depth or limited, there are a thousand questions for every organizational assessment. The key is to choose or create those questions that are most important to the organization under review.

The school principal may ask what happened to the many graduates of past years. The director of a company department may wonder if his competitors in other departments are really obtaining the performance they claim. An international development bank may want to know the prospects for success if the power sector is privatized. An international development agency may want to understand capacity needs in a targeted organization (NGO). A nation that contributes to a UN organization wants to know if it is getting its money's worth.

Lists of questions are easy to generate, but mapping those questions is very difficult, and holds the key to successful assessment. Typically, this part of the assessment process is poorly done, despite it being the most critical element for starting on the right track.

Before addressing specific questions, the issue of hidden agendas and how they relate to organizational assessments needs to be considered. Often, the decision to do some type of review is motivated by perceptions of problems within the organization. Governing boards or funders may suspect poor performance, and they may have prejudged the reasons that generally relate to personnel performance issues. The sponsors may view organizational assessment as a means of obtaining a better understanding of the situation without transparently acknowledging the suspected problem. Certainly, an effective organizational assessment can fill in the available data, but it should not be considered a substitute for management or performance reviews.

The organizational assessment framework provides a useful structure to examine the questions that need to be asked. It also indicates the scope of concerns, and provides the reviewers with a reference that ensures that all relevant facets of the assessment were addressed. While the emphasis of an assessment may vary from situation to situation, having a framework provides an overall map that serves as a useful starting point. As noted earlier, generating a large number of questions is not difficult. What is challenging is to reduce the list to the essence. The table above lists generic questions at the most general level for an organizational assessment. That list of questions becomes much longer when sub-questions are added. What, then, are the most important questions? Essentially, all four aspects of performance must be understood, and then as much of the other dimensions as required to understand how performance is being influenced or could be enhanced. Approaches to questions in each of the four dimensions follow.

Framing Performance Questions

Performance is the paramount theme and should be included in every organizational assessment. The first consideration in analyzing performance in an organization is to understand how people view performance. Unless people are clear and agree on the definition of performance, reviewers and internal stakeholders will disagree on the conclusions of an assessment, because they approach performance from differ-

---

EXAMPLES OF ORGANIZATIONAL PERFORMANCE ISSUES AND INDICATORS

PERFORMANCE DIMENSION	ISSUES	INDICATORS
Effectiveness	■ The mission is being accomplished	■ Literacy rates ■ Level of access to schools
Efficiency	■ Maximal use is made of physical facilities (buildings, equipment)	■ Cost per client served ■ Program completion rates
Relevance	■ Stakeholders attitude towards organization ■ Stakeholder needs assessments are conducted regularly	■ Stakeholder satisfaction (clients, donors, etc.) ■ Number of supporters, subscribers, funders
Financial viability	■ The organization has diversified funding ■ Existing funding sources offer sustained support	■ Percentage of funding by source

ing perspectives. There are two requirements: the issues and indicators of performance, and the importance placed on them. Note that there are both issues and indicators, since sometimes what is required is an analysis (issue) that does not reduce to a simplistic indicator. In other cases, indicators give the data needed for analysis.

Importance can be ascertained by reducing the issues or indicators to a small number (one to three per dimension). Often, the realities of available data dictate what indicators can be included, at least the first time an organization is involved with assessment. It is better to concentrate on easily obtainable data and complete the assessment in a timely manner than to spend many months trying to find elusive data. An organizational assessment is just a picture at a point in time. The analysis can, and should, go on in subsequent assessments. If people limit their issues and indicators in this way, it is relatively easy to see what is important. There are situations where diverse stakeholders cannot agree. If the differences cannot be resolved, there is no basis for an assessment that will be endorsed by the different stakeholders, so an inclusive process is out of the question.

PERFORMANCE ANALYSIS

An organizational assessment of a Lithuanian liberal arts college included consideration of how the donor's funds contributed to the college's state of development. The college offers a four-year English language undergraduate program in several majors, including business. The indicators used for effectiveness included market demand for the college's programs, employability of graduates, positive reputation of the college, and student and alumni quality assessments. The first two were quantitative indicators, whereas the latter two were qualitative. Relevance issues included analysis of the fit between a Western liberal arts curriculum and the needs of an evolving market economy; the relationship of a North American business curriculum to the realities of business in post-Communist Lithuania; and the college's efforts to adapt its curriculum as secondary school graduates became more fluent in English, the language of instruction.

There were two efficiency indicators. The first was student completion rates. It was found that because of environmental factors, a third of the students did not complete the four-year program. However, we were unable to judge whether this represented good or bad performance, given that some students left before graduation due to market demand. The second indicator was the cost of faculty salaries relative to the overall budget. Finally, financial viability was reduced to two indicators: net income, and diversity of funding sources. Using this limited list of issues and indicators, we were able to understand performance in its four dimensions.

Questions that Deal with Capacity

Capacity needs to be understood in terms of its relationship to performance, rather than in response to the wants of people inside the organization. Capacity questions lend themselves to both norm referencing and criterion referencing. Norm referenced approaches compare capacities to benchmarks within similar organizations or industries. This enables reviewers to make comparative judgments once they know the answers to certain questions. For example, what span of control do managers have? What is the ratio of support staff to professionals? What are the cash reserves? How many computers of each type are available? By comparing the answers to averages or best practices, reviewers can make judgments about capacity and its adequacy.

We acknowledge that in many cases, there are no readily available benchmarks. Experienced organizational assessment teams may have access to relevant comparisons that inexperienced teams do not. However, if no benchmarks are available, there must either be an investment in order to collect them, or else the assessment must do without them by using the baseline approach with comparisons over time.

A criterion-referenced approach uses conventions that reflect values for capacity. For example, organizations sometimes refer to standards for such measures as the ratio of support staff to managers, the proportion of staff with stated qualifications, the number of staff who have access to a computer, and so forth. The best developed are standards (such as ISO) that prescribe the necessary requirements for an organization to achieve recognition for meeting the standard.

LINKING CAPACITY AND PERFORMANCE

The Lithuanian college example shows how key capacity issues linked to performance can be addressed easily. In that case, the college has a new building, a well-endowed library and computer infrastructure, which are far ahead of other educational organizations in that country. Positive performance in relevance was linked to a responsive and evolving governance structure with strategic leadership. We considered student faculty ratios when we assessed capacity. They were about 17:1, which compares adequately to North American benchmarks, but is far higher than the 4:1 ratio of universities in Lithuania. The ratios were appropriate, as the college had high performance in both efficiency and cost-effectiveness. Capacity limitations were found, however, in one academic program that lacked qualified faculty, in some of the university's linkages to other colleges, and in financial management systems. Thus, the organizational assessment identified some priorities in capacity development that we believe will lead to better performance of the college.

Motivational Issues and Questions

Assessing motivation is extremely challenging because individuals are complex. Place these people together within groups and organizations and the challenges multiply. Measuring motivation is similar to trying to assess community values—difficult to define, but you know them when you see them. To say that an organization is suffering from malaise is not hard, and may not even be contested; however, to represent this presents difficulties. There are corporate culture instruments that can help, and some of them permit comparisons that position the dimensions of culture relative to norms. It is also often helpful to use qualitative approaches and provide anecdotes, vignettes or quotes to illustrate employee attitudes about their organization.

The crucial consideration in assessing motivation is to understand the types of issues and corresponding data that stakeholders understand. Often, a single event or series of events can have profound effects on the overall motivation of a department, region or the entire organization. For example, one insensitive manager can provoke an entire staff, which in turn has a profound effect on the way work is done and how the organization operates. At the individual level, staff is often personally affected by unfair criticism or, on the other end of the spectrum, by receiving praise.

Asking employees for their impressions of the organization often captures the essence of motivation. Such comments as: "The best place I have ever worked," or "We are the leader in our field," suggest a motivation that supports the mission.

Determining What Needs to Be Known about the Environment

We all understand that the environment influences every organization. It exerts expectations on an organization's ability to achieve its mission, it provides limits on its degrees of freedom, it dictates financial subsidies, and it provides rules of the game that bracket organizational development. Furthermore, the environment can be described in both qualitative and quantitative terms. The challenge for the reviewer is to analyze the extent to which environmental forces positively and negatively impact the organization. While certain environments may make achieving positive performance difficult, it is not hard to identify examples of organizations that prospered despite a challenging environment.

Organizational Assessment Methodology

The organizational assessment approach outlined in the previous chapters sets forth a framework and a set of questions that—with the proper data, analysis and judgments—can lead to a better understanding of the organization and its performance. However, as implied above, the choice of methods used to design the assessment, collect data and select questions raises some series issues.

Basically, organizational assessment follows in the tradition of a methodology known as a "case study." A case study is a qualitative form of assessment, though it uses both qualitative and quantitative data. Case studies rely on multiple sources of information to gain insight into the organization (Anderson, 1998). In this methodological tradition, the emphasis is on understanding. In other words, in doing an organizational assessment based on the case study approach, the aim is to understand the meaning of a question. There is no a priori answer being tested. The assessment is trying to understand existing capacities and how they affect the performance of the organization under review.

A case study approach requires identifying the sources of information, the instruments to use, and the ways to collect information, as well as analyzing the information. The sections that follow summarize these tasks.

Sources of Data

Six sources of evidence are typically used in conducting case studies: documentation, file data, interviews, site visits, direct observation, and physical artifacts. For most organizational assessment questions, some type of documentation is generally available, including reports, file data, memoranda and previous studies. Interviews are

---

MISSION STATEMENTS ARE IMPORTANT

A recent assessment of a graduate school in a university supported with technical assistance funds from a foreign donor asked about the project's mission statement. The project director stated that there was one, but he could not find it when interviewed. Neither could he recall the specific content of the statement. What was significant, then, was that the director did not consider the mission statement to be central to the organization, despite the fact that the content of the statement, once it was located, was judged to be relevant and sound.

---

prime sources of data for assessments. Not only do we interview a range of respondents, we also try to find key informants who have inside knowledge of what is going on. These individuals are critical to enhancing the validity of the conclusions drawn.

Surveys are often used in organizational assessments to gather data from a large number of organizational members. This is particularly important in assessing organizational culture and process issues. Typically, an assessment requires on-site visits for direct observations, which can be very helpful for understanding why things are as suggested by other data sources. Finally, physical artifacts should not be overlooked; some assessors even systematically checks bulletin boards (electronic ones in some organizations) to help understand the organizational culture.

Typical data sources that might be helpful to an organizational assessment include a table of company milestones, that is, dates and events that help in an understanding of the organization, changes in leadership, the introduction of new programs, and construction activities. For organizational structure, it might be helpful to locate present and past organigrams, staff lists, minutes of meetings, policy handbooks, regulations, and perhaps even a diagram of the physical plant. Organizations have lots of data, and the assessor needs to have the experience to choose sources that best answer the key questions.

Data Collection

As in any methodology, assessment requires a work plan that defines what will be done, and how and when it will be done. Organizational assessments tend to be a method of immersion. An important aspect of data collection is the creation of various study databases. Weak assessments generally confuse the data with its reporting, whereas the best ones maintain a separate inventory of data with charts, tables and numbers, some of which are used in the text. Other information is appended, while still other information is not used at all.

Data Analysis

The masses of data potentially available for organizational assessments can present insurmountable problems, unless the assessors know what types of analysis are required. Our assessments provide a categorization system or framework that significantly eases the issues of data analysis. For example, if you were exploring issues of structure, you would separate out data related to Board governance from data related to operations. In both instances, you might want to explore such issues as the clarity of roles and authority.

It is at the data gathering and analysis stages that important insights emerge. This is usually a good moment for the team to test assumptions and conclusions. It is important to understand that in a case study as used in organizational analysis, the analysis phase takes place as the data are collected. The opportunity to test conclusions in the field is an advantage of this methodology.

Some Key Issues

Expertise

In general, organizational assessments are complex and require a variety of people with differing expertise to successfully complete them. Ideally, they are carried out by a team with collective skills and a strong leader with a clear vision of the task. Intelligent, well-rounded people with diverse experience and solid research and evaluation skills make the best reviewers, providing the team includes the necessary content expertise representative of the field of the organization under study. Interestingly, one of the most respected institutions for studies on public health, the Institute of Medicine, does not use researchers on its evaluation teams who are expert in the specific area of research being assessed (Stoto, 1997). This contributes to freshness in perspective. One strong advantage of a team, however, is that it can capitalize on the collective strengths, rather than rely on one individual who is always a compromise among stakeholder interests.

There are many sources of analytic and evaluation expertise and many views concerning what type of expertise has value. It depends largely on the purpose of the

---

APPEARANCES CAN BE DECEIVING

The client of one recent evaluation had received a complaint regarding an evaluation we had helped conduct of the book publishing industry in Canada. An industry leader took exception to our having interviewed a well-known industry gadfly because of concerns that we had been "taken in" by his extreme views. Our attempt to be objective and accepting of all perspectives was mistakenly interpreted as acquiescence.

organizational assessment and its client. Considerations in choosing reviewers include credibility, expertise and distance from the organization under review. Credibility is crucial, and different stakeholders have differing credibility criteria. Most staff in an organization want to involve respected content experts, presumably because they feel their professional concerns cannot be adequately addressed by someone outside their profession, and because professional peers have the same socialization, and most likely, similar values. They also probably neither understand alternative professions for reviewers—such as a social scientist, economist or evaluator—nor know what they might offer to the task. Even if there is a predilection to relevant professional content, content is not sufficient by itself.

Often the client of an organizational assessment requires evaluation expertise. The evaluation expert has methodological expertise, and may be more technically competent, not to mention more independent and objective in raising certain questions. But he or she is often suspect in terms of credibility due to a lack of professional content expertise.

Whose Perspective? External and Internal Reviewers

In both the analytic and evaluation approaches, the output is a function of your vantage point for viewing the problem, which is the distance between the reviewer and the organization being assessed. The most proximate reviewers are members of the organization whose involvement on an organizational assessment team can either be advantageous or a liability to operations and to objectivity. These people can save a lot of background research by presenting ready information about the organization and its existing data. Involvement of organization members is often helpful for the analytic approach.

However, in accountability evaluations, as Chelimsky and North discovered in their evaluation of the Global Environmental Facility, too much loosely structured involvement of internal stakeholders with vested interests creates conflicts over agendas, methodologies, working relationships and the wording of reports (North, 1997). As a result of the experience, North concluded that it is essential to have an evaluation coordinator acceptable to all parties, clear and unfettered reporting relationships within the team, a common script or report outline for sub-components, and trust and mutual respect among the evaluators and in the evaluators' relationships with stakeholders.

Another consideration is the need for sufficient distance to avoid "insight fatigue" that is sometimes associated with people who spent many years viewing the organization from a single perspective. Keep in mind that an insider's position on issues is generally known, so he or she cannot be neutral or perceived to be objective in making judgments. Furthermore, if an organization shows signs of fracturing through cliques and cabals, an insider may have difficulty getting people from other camps to confide, or at the very least, have difficulty giving their contributions credence. Returning to what skills and knowledge a reviewer requires, the insider needs these in abundance if he or she is to successfully overcome the potential objectivity problems that result from being too close to what is being assessed.

STRENGTHS AND WEAKNESSES IN REVIEWERS

	STRENGTHS	**WEAKNESSES**
Internal reviewers	■ Know the organization ■ Link organizational assessment to organizational change	■ Presence may convey political messages ■ Insight fatigue ■ Inability to criticize superiors ■ Organization can't let them go
External reviewers	■ Can specify expertise requirements ■ Viewed as independent ■ Can focus on the organizational assessment	■ Don't know the organization and the available data ■ May have to limit site presence due to cost

All this considered, the central issue is the extent to which one actually wants an approach that provides an independent and credible organizational assessment that incorporates the highest ethical standards. The purist position as held by Michael Scriven (1997) asserts that with such ethical standards, an evaluator is capable of objectivity, but to be objective, he or she must avoid being too close. Scriven suggests that even such procedures as staff interviews reduce distance and compromise objectivity because the human face of the organization that may be hurt if a negative view is conveyed may influence the assessment. To the critics of this stance who believe that there is no objectivity, he says "the public is less naïve and thinks that regulatory agencies that socialize with those they regulate should be viewed with suspicion, as judges think the same about jurors socializing with defense attorneys" (Scriven, 1997, p. 487).

The role of the head of the organization depends on the person and the context for the assessment. Heads of departments, permanent secretaries or other organization heads often wisely prefer to maintain some distance to ensure they are not seen as overly influencing the process. However, when the process involves more future oriented diagnoses, or initiatives for strategic change, it is preferable that the organization's leader be involved.

Self-Assessment

Self-assessment is part of what has recently been termed "empowerment evaluation," which is defined as the use of evaluation concepts, techniques and findings to foster improvement and self-determination (Fetterman, Kaftarian and Wandersman, 1996). This approach embraces an unambiguous value orientation, for it is designed to help people help themselves and improve their organizations and programs using a form of self-evaluation and reflection. Self-assessment embraces organizational development and change questions and is highly applicable when the purpose is organizational development. Involving organizational members provides a direct link to implementation by providing them with data and assessment findings.

One major consideration is the cost-benefit of taking people from their own areas of expertise and involving them in something they need to learn at an opportunity cost to their normal duties. This is a political decision generally made by the head of the organization, who sees the assessment as advancing the organization's strategic goals. Needless to say, the best results come from involving the most respected and competent staff—the very ones who typically are already making the largest organizational contributions.

Is organizational self-assessment worth the trouble? This is a critical question. On the positive side, this form of reflective practice can deepen stakeholder insight into an organization—its strengths and weaknesses, motivation and performance. But, on the negative side, at the best of times, it takes considerable time and energy. Can an organization afford to involve its personnel in such an extravagance? Can it afford not to? Furthermore, is it an opportune time to stir the emotions of staff about the certain shortcomings that will be raised? Is the organization and its staff prepared to act on the information that will be revealed? Some leaders are confident in their own leadership and welcome new insights. Others are more circumspect. Maybe there are other critical challenges at this juncture. Maybe staff are at odds with the administration; maybe it is best to leave sleeping dogs lie—at least for now.

Engaging in organizational self-assessment raises two important issues. First, is it the best means to achieve organizational development? At times it may be, and at other times not. The organization may need a common task in which to engage people in thinking about the organization. If so, a self-assessment may be an answer. On the other hand, the organization's staff are not professional reviewers, and they may have only rudimentary skills, resulting in a costly, imperfect and potentially damaging exercise.

The second issue is validity. Because the purpose of self-assessment is organizational development, validity may be less of a concern than with accountability evaluation. However, you often find the assessment attempting to serve both purposes. For example, development assistance donors that fund organizations need accountability, but the organization is interested in self-assessment, so often the agendas end up combined. There are safeguards to validity, such as the use of external reviewers, but it is nevertheless difficult to combine processes with such different purposes. The evaluation approach focuses on how well the organization is performing, whereas the analytic approach may be more interested in how it can improve. One recommendation is to use a two-level structure that first enables the organization to conduct some or all the elements of a self-assessment for its purpose, and then uses this as data for an external assessment (Anderson and Gilsig, 1998).

In deciding whether to engage in self-assessment, it is helpful to have a sense of the context. We have seen instances where employees tried to hijack an organizational assessment for their own ends. We also experienced situations where staff were highly critical of their leader, but were not in a favorable position to communicate their displeasure. In all such contexts, self-assessment should be avoided. It is more advisable to use external teams that are impartial and can deliver the messages without tracing them to particular people on the inside.

The only way a self-assessment can be really useful in organizational development is if the leader fully supports or even leads it. There have been instances, however, where the leader adopted self-assessment merely to be in a position to control the agenda and process. In other words, the leader was inclined to support it as a less risky alternative to external assessment. If there are external reviewers involved, this can work, but it is still only an approximation of a valid organizational assessment. Arnold Love (1991, p. 7) put it well when he wrote:

> The manager is a believer in people and programs, a partisan advocate and supporter; by contrast, the evaluator is a doubter who is uncommitted to anything or anyone. Finally, the manager is warm and outgoing, a leader and part of a team, as the evaluator sits in perpetual shade, cool and aloof, a lone wolf detached from the pack.

Qualitative and Quantitative Data

Categorically speaking, data are either quantitative (numeric) or qualitative (non-numeric). Some analysts and evaluators prefer quantitative data. For example, analysts are adept at collecting and interpreting financial data on performance—that is, hard quantitative data. Performance indicators such as return on investment can tell a great deal about an organization, but considered in isolation, such data may fail to capture the underlying upstream reasons for the result. Increased return on investment may be a result of asset depletion or short-term benefits from a management intervention such as borrowing. These indicators, while robust, may have other problems. In government and civil society organizations, it is often difficult to capture their results in economic terms alone. If an NGO's purpose is to empower civil society, for example, economic results may be the wrong indicator; however, appropriate quantitative indicators are often difficult to agree upon.

Qualitative data incorporates a reviewer's judgment on its saliency for the assessment. It represents relevance that goes beyond mere counts. There are social reasons for having a university or a hospital that are not reflected in quantifiable measures of performance. Another example is the strength of environment factors, such as the political context. How do you judge the political climate and the effect on the organization under review? Or the cultural values and ethos and their effect on the labor market and, ultimately, the organization? Qualitative data and analysis provides some insight into these concerns.

In the debate over the relative merits of quantitative and qualitative data, the compromise position would seem to incorporate both. While we advocate this position, there are risks, most particularly having a suitable balance with the importance of each data type. It is easy to be in a position of doing neither type of data justice, and being condemned by both quantitative and qualitative adherents. The fact is that people with differing values and orientations have different views about the type of data that they feel is important.

Data Sources

Typical data sources include documents, people and databases. Obviously, documents need to be reviewed based on their authorship, and with an understanding of the original context and purpose for which they were written.

People represent special challenges, either when involved in normative data collection subject to quantitative analysis, or for their qualitative insights. Two of the most common issues are including a proper sample, and ensuring that the data collected are valid or truthful. Sampling is always problematic. Do you include former staff, as well as the present guard? Are critics of an organization identified for inclusion? In some approaches, such as economic analysis, people may be excluded altogether, though possibly at a political cost. Indeed, many donor agencies review their investments without direct contact with the people involved except on a project sample basis.

Turning to the other issue, it is always challenging to understand what people are conveying and to assess the degree of bias in their statements. Instrumentation problems can arise, especially when questionnaires and interviews are conducted in cross-cultural environments. When collecting non-numeric data from people, vetting, pilot-testing and other forms of validation may be required for data collection instruments. One of the costs of the trend toward self-assessment and internal eval-

---

IN WHOSE INTEREST?

The Canadian province of Ontario has launched a satisfaction survey of college graduates, but it also includes feedback from employers. The government will adjust the size of college grants according to these perceptions of performance. Are the benchmarks a useful way to make judgments? How do the survey results control for self-interest?

uation is neglecting the fundamental requirements of the reliability and validity of data collection techniques because people do not understand the importance, or they lack the requisite technical skills. This underscores the advisability of defining indicators and data collection procedures on an ongoing basis, rather than just when a formal organizational assessment takes place.

One of the most difficult people challenges is in knowing how to value data that are distorted by self-interest, be it highly praiseworthy, or unreasonably negative. Missing data are particularly troublesome unless reviewers take the trouble to investigate why people do not respond. People who benefit from an organization's programs tend to be positive in their assessments. They may have selected the program, and negative comments reflect on their own choice. If they obtained a financial benefit such as an income-support payment or scholarship, they tend to say: "Great, but more money would have been better." Validity can also be enhanced through triangulation.

Another people issue is how much data are enough within the value-laden environment of an assessment. It matters little if statisticians agree that 100 questionnaires to consumers of an organization's services are sufficient if the political environment requires hearing from 1,000. Credibility is of as much concern as statistical validity. Thus, if stakeholders are consulted at all, it is imperative that the assessment be seen as inclusive and as providing all stakeholders with a voice.

Databases are another source of information, and we need to understand the sources and collection procedures for the data provided. It is important to check if statistical data are out of date and may be suspect in terms of reliability and validity. Once the data are captured, you need to ensure that new errors do not creep in when different software is used, or when transforming and combining is required. It should be noted that most organizations have a great deal of internally generated data such as financial system data that can be invaluable for assessment. Regrettably, many organizations do not fully understand the link between budget categories and performance, so sometimes these data are not in categories that facilitate efficient analysis. In certain cases, the use of externally generated data, such as industry benchmarking, can be of value to organizational assessment. For example, consulting or accountant fee revenues can be quoted in multiples of daily salary, and reflect the industry norms.

Validity

The principal methodological challenge of organizational assessment is validity. Validity has three principal issues: 1) false assertion of a positive result; 2) failure to detect a positive result; and 3) asking the wrong questions and contaminating the assessment with organizational or personal bias (Dunn, 1982).

There are many reasons for problems with validity. Organizations are seen as trying their best to do good things, so reviewers "go looking for" rather than just "go looking." Furthermore, the way questions are framed, upstream perspectives, the way data are collected, and non-response problems build in a bias toward reports of positive performance. The involvement of reviewers close to the organization confounds objectivity. Not-for-profit organizations that do not have a bottom line result in biased judgments in the absence of baselines or benchmarks. It is overly easy to conclude that an organization is doing good things when it is assisting the poor, or building democracy, or housing the homeless—but it is much harder to judge whether it is doing all that it could with its available resources.

Errors also occur when the assessment is restricted in time and resources, such as when reviewers are not able to visit consumers or access other primary data sources. Results may also be missed if by nature they are long term. Organizations that deal with complex effects such as community development may sow the seeds for results that do not occur for a decade. Similarly, educational organizations that may spend years delivering education services cannot be assessed completely until their graduates have years of work experience.

Finally, errors occur because reviewers may be biased or blind to the questions that need to be asked. In multilateral donor-supported ministries, agencies and organizations, this can be a central question. In an evaluation of the Tanzania Railways Project, it was discovered that the railroad was now largely redundant, given the rise of more cost-effective trucking on an improved network of roads. Professional ethics suggest that evaluators are obliged to pose such questions even if they are not included in the terms of reference, though this may not be the case for team members who are not professional evaluators.

The two ways to counter this validity limitation involve the use of benchmarks or baseline comparisons. Benchmarking enables an organization to compare itself to standards in the industry. This is particularly useful when performance indicators are compared, such as return on investment, cost of haulage per ton-mile, gross margin, or agricultural yield per hectare. Valid measurement techniques can lead to agreement on the data. The interpretation of differences becomes the analytic issue, because the cause of the observed differences needs to be attribute to sources within or outside the organization. The comparisons are only valid when the benchmarks are considered applicable, which is often not the case or even possible across countries that may have different policy and economic environments. It may also not be possible across geographic regions that may have all kinds of different conditions. One type of benchmarking—accreditation—is used in some social sectors such as health and education. Organizations are accredited if they conform to certain standards of capacity, and sometimes performance.

Reviewers who change hats following the assessment and assume the role of facilitators or performance consultants are viewed by some as being in conflict of interest, since they can be perceived as consciously or unconsciously orienting the report to promote their services (Scriven, 1997). Internal reviewers may similarly orient the organization according to their future role within it.

Given all of these validity concerns, the major issue for reviewers is to consider for whose interests they are working. Is it the client? The people who pay for the organization? The organization? The consumers and beneficiaries of the organization? The courtroom may applaud what you say in presenting your case, but to win your case, you need to convince the judge.

THE REPORT:
COMMUNICATING THE RESULTS OF THE EXERCISE

The assessment is not complete until it is communicated or reported upon in some tangible form such as a printed report. Not that this is easy, because the printed word has a way of distorting what was intended. Nonetheless, written reports represent important organizational milestones, and serve as baselines for subsequent assessments. They also provide a sense of closure to the process and signify the time to move forward in acting on what was found. Michael Quinn Patton (1990)

> **CHARACTERISTICS OF USEFUL ORGANIZATIONAL ASSESSMENT REPORTS**
>
> ■ Written to reach specific defined audiences
> ■ Short but analytic (how short and analytic depends on audience)
> ■ Reflect the four dimensions of performance
> ■ Compare the organization's characteristics to baselines and benchmarks
> ■ Provide recommendations and options to improve performance.

advocates a presentation and discussion rather than a formal report, which he feels is too symbolic and paternalistic. But not all reviewers share this view.

Reporting is never easy if you are to preserve integrity and also communicate. There are always issues with style and the need to conform to the client's expectations. Some agencies and clients want detail, while others want brevity. Some want extensive appendices, while some do not. We were recently involved in producing a report with what we considered to be highly informative graphs, only to learn that one of our clients had difficulty reading graphs and preferred tables. However, despite these challenges, a report says what should be said and hopefully makes it public—at least to those paying for the organizational assessment.

Reports go to audiences that are often diverse. An organizational assessment must serve the needs of the client, and theoretically should go to the client first. However, there are advantages to showing a preliminary draft to the organization, for it gives those directly involved a chance to correct incomplete or incorrect data before it becomes public. It also begins the process of softening the blow that a negative report will create.

Most assessments produce what is known as "report shock." It is the highly emotional reaction by the leaders of an organization when they first see a critical analysis that represents the organization in a way that is perceptually different from what is imagined. This is not unlike a personnel performance appraisal in which employees view themselves in highly positive terms, and then receive an objective contrary analysis backed up with data. This natural reaction needs to be managed or it can destroy the utility of an assessment report.

It is useful to allow the head of the organization to review the penultimate draft of the report with ample time to immediately meet with the assessment team to review the report and how it is worded. Often, re-wording a few sentences can do wonders for support of the analysis. Experience has taught us to be highly sensitive to the use of negative terms in the report itself. Terms like "not" provoke an understandable human reaction from people who have given a lot to an organization. In practice, it is beneficial to ask colleagues to review the findings and conclusions, and rate them as positive, negative and neutral. Too many negatives may call for re-wording if the report is to receive a fair hearing.

While the client is the audience that needs to be served, most reports go to other audiences as well. Certainly the organization receives the report, and in many cases comments on it. In some cases, the comments are incorporated as an appendix to the report. The difficulty for the author is to write a report that can be used and understood by different audiences. A good report speaks directly to its primary audience, though the organization should learn from it as well. Sometimes, the terms of reference provide for recommendations to the funder and the organization that are then identified in the report.

CONCLUSIONS

This chapter considered many of the issues that concern people interested in organizational assessment. Some concerns, however, were not addressed. Some concerns are methodological:

- How do you select a particular data collection methodology?
- How do you deal with data analysis when the data are distorted, incomplete or contradictory?
- How do you ensure that the data are sufficient? When do you stop?

These are the concerns of every social science researcher. These tend to be issues that require judgment based on experience or expertise. Researchers deal with them by doing as much as they can in an imperfect world. Those who have never done this type of work cannot be expected to know all the answers, so novices can be greatly assisted by teams of people with more experience.

Another set of concerns centers on the difficulties of organizational change:

- How do you overcome resistance to the assessment process?
- How do you determine which of the areas of organizational improvement are most important?
- How can organizational assessments best support performance?

These concerns require a different expertise and experience as to how to assist organizational development. There is both an art and a science that organizational development experts can share. While it is not possible to consider this in-depth here, the questions are important and suggest that organizational assessment must be more than a detached and passive research process. Without a dimension of organizational change, an assessment loses much of its rationale.

The best way to address people's concerns is to engage them in actual experience with the organizations with which they are most familiar. For all the limitations of the organizational assessment process, it does provide insights that were not previously apparent. It does this because of its systematic framework that helps include every important issue, and because of its philosophy of engagement. People who become involved in assessing organizations, even with partial and imperfect data, will benefit from understanding the dynamic of organizational performance.

Chapter Seven

IMPLEMENTING AN ORGANIZATIONAL ASSESSMENT

Over the last 30 years, international development practitioners and researchers have identified the central role that organizations and institutions play in improving the use of development assistance (Eaton,1972; Uphoff, 1972; Savedoff, 1998; Picciotto and Weisner, 1998). As discussed in the last chapter, most if not all development projects have their origin in situations where a particular organization or group of organizations have not been efficiently or effectively carrying out their mandate (discharging a function or providing a service), or want to improve their ability to discharge their mandate. In other words, they want to perform better.

It is therefore not surprising that most projects, besides providing direct programmatic assistance—hospitals receive funds to improve their "health mandate," educational institutions their "educational mandate"—also include institutional strengthening components.[1] Presumably designed to modernize or strengthen the organization in question, these components typically involve training managers, purchasing new equipment, updating accounting and financial systems, and implementing structural reforms.

Those suggesting these institutional changes have what Drucker (1995) calls a "theory of the firm." This is an implicit set of hypotheses or assumptions that characterize either how a firm is operating or how it should operate. For example, a review of 15 development projects for the Inter-American Development Bank dis-

---

[1] In our review of development projects, support for both organizations and institutions is put under a category called "institutional strengthening." The more subtle distinction between institution and organization made in this book does not usually occur in development projects.

cerned a pattern in which the accounting system of the agency executing the loan was always updated. The implicit assumption is that such systems will improve the financial controls, reporting and efficiency of both the executing agents and, in some instances, the organization. The assumptions and theories held by organizational members and development practitioners are operationalized through the process of organizational diagnosis, creation of projects or programs, and implementation of the project or program.

In this book, we have put forth a diagnostic framework used to articulate and make more transparent some of our ideas linked to a "theory" of how to improve the performance of organizations. From the perspective of our framework, every development investment is a test of a set of hypotheses about organizational change and performance improvement. Basically, our "theory of the firm" sets forth that organizational performance is a function of the environment within which the organization exists, its capacities, and its motivation. Any planned change to the environment, capacity or motivation of the organization occurs because of an implicit change theory.

If an organization or an investor (development agency) wants to change the performance of an organization—for example, increase the ability of the Ministry of Education to provide basic skills to students—then a diagnosis is undertaken and a series of hypotheses are developed and translated into some action. A project in this context is a deliberate act to improve performance. The ultimate purpose of a project undertaken by an organization is to improve organizational performance in the areas identified.

Over the past decade, there have been many new development innovations at the management, institutional and other levels aimed at improving the performance of development organizations. These include interventions such as total quality management, re-engineering, privatization, decentralization and performance management.

There are assumptions or hypotheses about how organizational change takes place, and in this context, the framework helps describe the rationale and potential logic for future donor investments. As aid continues to be questioned, and as we search for ways to communicate results, the gap between rich and poor countries grows, and global social and health problems spill over national borders. The search for better ways to organize and improve organizational performance becomes more pressing. To make our implicit assumptions and hypotheses more explicit, this chapter speculates about the use of the framework to create change and examines how we can learn to better intervene in organizations. The intent in this final chapter is not to summarize what we have already said, but to offer some observations about the use of the framework. This includes addressing the concerns cited below, all of which affect the diagnosis of an organization and how the diagnosis is used.

1) The concern about ownership is crucial to undertaking an organizational assessment. An important underlying hypothesis of the assessment is that the organization being evaluated is interested in using the results to improve itself. To do this requires paying attention to the issue of ownership. Who owns the results of the organizational assessment? Who is creating the hypotheses for change?

2) Related to ownership is the concern that organizational assessments can become "ceremonial" events to reinforce the status quo. This occurs when organizational members want to avoid the change orientation and transparency that an organizational assessment implies.

3) The concern about the use of "projects" as the primary vehicle to support and change organizations. Projects may distort the organization if they are not carried out within the context of an organizational performance framework—what we refer to as the project "trap."

4) The concern about the timing of organizational assessments, particularly the need to consider the link between the organization and its "life cycle stage." This involves the leadership, organizational and economic cycles, since they play key roles in the success of an assessment and in the meaning of the findings.

5) The concern about the link between logic models and organizational assessments. Here, we raise the issue of recognizing the need for dynamic use of the logical framework. Furthermore, we point to the need to recognize that a project logic and performance system might not be the same as one that helps improve organizational performance.

6) Finally, the concern about the application of existing diagnostic frameworks (such as the one presented in this book) and new organizational forms such as membership organizations and inter-organizational groups (networks, consortia, etc.) that may require different types of assessment. Many of these organizational forms have fuzzy boundaries, unclear ownership, and, in whole or in part, may be temporary structures. These characteristics can greatly alter the assessment in terms of the questions asked and the priority given to certain areas.

Organizational Assessment and Ownership

Organizational assessment is driven by both accountability and learning. From an accountability perspective, it may be required to demonstrate the performance of the organization to a donor, a licensing body, or a boss. This could either be to ensure continuity of a funding or licensing arrangement, or a new level of licensing. It may also be part of assessing a new phase of support. While such an assessment may result in organizational learning and change, that is not the main issue. The main issue is to determine the merit of the organization as part of a decision (usually external to the organization) about some aspect of the organization's funding or permission to operate.

Learning and knowledge also drive organizational assessment. Assessment provides a vehicle to better understand how an organization is functioning. While many of the questions in the organizational diagnosis remain the same as in accountability assessment, the intent is to internally use the information to move beyond a picture of the current state and to make operational decisions about how to improve the organization.

Our priority and concern is about the use of assessment for organizational improvement, and we situate ourselves in the "knowledge" more than the "accountability" areas. We are concerned with issues such as how to make assessments more relevant to building knowledge that contributes to learning and improved organizational performance.

Our experience indicates that it is critical to look at who is defining and conducting an organizational assessment. If the assessment is carried out by a licensing body through a donor or a project implementation unit, it is generally unsuccessful in contributing to improved performance. This is consistent with findings over the last 40 years in development assistance. Those responsible must feel a sense of ownership—a commitment to success.

Ownership is associated with several factors that make up the organizational assessment. Staff members need to have the capacity to benefit from the work of the organization. They need to gain skills, change systems that inhibit successful work, and have an incentive system that supports processes of change. In sum, staff members need the commitment and ownership to stay with the change process. Ownership is important both at the leadership level as well as at the ground level where actions are carried out and decisions taken. One of the lessons learned from our previous work is that the data generated in the assessment needs to be seen as valid both at the top and at the bottom of the organization.

This often presents a paradox in development work. When the results of an external assessment deem that the existing organization is not capable of managing the loan and the related work, a project support or implementation unit is recommended as a mechanism to carry out the project. Project implementation units are established to avoid organizational and institutional shortcomings of the sponsoring organization that could, it is felt, result in delays, cost overruns or outright failure.

Thus a typical implementation unit has greater access to decision makers, such as the minister, and are exempt for normal procurement procedures. They are also able to attract qualified staff with better salary and benefit packages than the sponsoring organization can offer—all factors that speed up project implementation.

While the idea of an implementation unit is appealing from the project point of view, there is abundant literature and experience to support the notion that teams fail when they are not part of the organization in which they are attempting to produce change, or when the organization does not have full ownership of the change process. As stated in a report on project execution by the Inter-American Development Bank (2000, p. 21):

> Project implementation units sometimes operate as enclaves in the overall system, and frequently do not assist, and in some cases, may even undermine the ability of executing agencies to subsequently manage project resources during the operational phase (which is generally when benefits materialize). Thus, a project financed by the Bank may have been implemented satisfactorily, but may not be sustainable in the long run, because underlying institutional problems have not been resolved. This is, and should be, a matter of concern to the Bank and to borrowers, since project completion is only a necessary—but not sufficient—condition for fulfilling overall development objectives.

This example suggests that relatively autonomous project implementation units can lack institutional and organizational commitment. They are therefore only successful in project terms, not in terms of enhancing the performance of the organiza-tion that will have to carry on the work after the project is closed if it is to have a last-ing impact. When the organizations that define and contribute to development in a society are circumvented because of their weaknesses, whether perceived or actual, a series of mechanisms are then created that further weaken the central organiza-tions and reduce their ability to effectively participate in the governance process.

How to break this vicious cycle is critical in the ownership discussion. The inclu-sion of key interests (leadership staff, board, clients, partners) in appropriate ways is essential if these groups are to integrate the lessons from the project into their ongoing development work. In other words, how can the organizational assessment support ownership and commitment to a process of change?

We believe that an assessment aimed at improving performance has to be car-ried out by key organizational members who have some responsibility for the actions of the organization. When a diagnosis of an organization is conducted, it is impor-tant that the people involved in the day-to-day workings of the organization be directly involved in the process. They need to see the assessment of problems as their own diagnosis. Any ideas on "why things work or don't work" should come from them. This way, they can create a hypothesis as to what is right or wrong in their own words, using their own thoughts and common sense (Weick, 1995).

If people do not own the organizational analysis, be it good or bad, they will not buy into any possible solution. Where some may say that the problem is always one of too little money, others who have taken the time to "own" the situation might be inclined to characterize the problem in a way that might lead to a solution. The prob-lem then becomes theirs, as does the responsibility for helping to solve it.

Ceremonial Assessments

Assessing organizational performance often means that some individuals gain and others lose. It is therefore a sensitive and highly political process in which managers, in particular, but others as well, may open themselves up to criticism and punish-ment. Those incentives often lead to avoiding open assessment of organizational performance. This can result in a "ceremonial assessment"—the steps are undertak-en, but in a very controlled manner, so that data is not released beyond the offices of a few individuals, and the report is carefully worded to keep all criticisms hidden.

An assessment of an organization should be a process of learning for all of the parties involved. An assessment should not be conducted just because someone, somewhere, says that it should be done. An assessment is a large investment of time, money, resources and, most importantly, people. An organization must be ready both to do the assessment and to accept its results.

There are also instances when it is in the interest of the leader of the organization to keep the analysis of performance fuzzy. The leader controls the dialogue and discourse during the assessment. When queried on certain matters, the response is often "You do not understand 'our organization'."

But when organizations are transparent, the power relationship changes. Organizational assessments open up dialogue. They can bring new actors into the organizational power structure and bring about other positive changes. Sometimes organizational members or even project implementing units do not see such transparency as helpful. Change works against their interests. In such a situation, organizational readiness is in question. Those engaged in assessments must pay attention to this pernicious occurrence.

The issue is how to get those in power to participate in the assessment and use its results. The process and the findings have to be carried out in such a manner that there is positive benefit for both the individuals involved and for development of the organization as a whole.

As part of determining how to start the assessment and maintain its momentum, there needs to be careful consideration of the control of the resources necessary for the organization's operation. This includes examining the resources controlled by management, external forces (donors, legislation, regulation), clients and staff, as well as considering how the assessment will affect each of these groups and how to generate a positive impact for all the interests involved. This does not mean that in every case everyone will be happy, or that there will be no organizational changes that result in management and staff changes. Rather, it means that it is essential to consider all these factors in the decision to design and implement an assessment to avoid or manage any undermining of the process by those who feel threatened. In some situations, this could mean delaying the assessment.

Investing in Organizational Performance: The Project Trap

Is the project the best way to think about enhancing organizational performance? Are we not at risk of losing sight of the bigger questions: To what extent does the project support or limit the performance of that organization? Are conditions better? Are people more capable in decision making? In creating new societies? In building local development?

In a recent survey of evaluations in South Asia, the International Development Research Centre found a significant lack of emphasis on the organizational capacities of the partners, and a strong emphasis on the results of the projects themselves (Bajaj, 1997). The recipient organizations found this frustrating because the evaluations were primarily useful to talk about the success or failure of the project, rather than how the project supported the mission or performance of the organization. In fact, the project was the focal point of interest, not the learning needs of the implementing organizations.

Project support creates potential problems and paradoxes for organizations. On the one hand, they need funded projects to exist; on the other, the project too often becomes more important than the organization. When projects are the primary focus of action and performance measurement, development organizations lose sight of the more complex performance requirements of the implementing organization. In some cases, the organizations become fragmented and feel they have lost their sense of direction in responding to the requirements of a range of donor partners. They can become trapped by their own success and stand at risk of serious organizational decline.

Investment, then, is defined and measured in terms of individual projects. What our experience tells us, however, is that projects distort when they are carried out without due consideration of the organizational performance framework of the implementing organization. While projects are important to organizations, they must be seen as contributing to overall long-term organizational performance.

A critical future challenge is to find ways to address this issue while respecting the needs of donors and international financial institutions in terms of accountability. This might include shifting the notion of accountability to include a stronger focus on the sustainability of efforts after the departure of the donor. While most donors already have this view of sustainability, the concept could be operationalized by focusing on investment in organizational performance.

A project is neither an organizational nor an investment model. As organizations struggle to find resources, the project should be seen as an intervention to aid the organization in its performance. Frequently, we have seen how projects upset an organization's equilibrium. Leaders are drawn into power struggles to try to meet the stated objectives of the project, thus causing disharmony within the organization.

The inclusion of primary project objectives related to the performance of the implementing organization could help to shift the focus of work from the project alone to its impact on the capacity of the organization to perform effectively over the long term. If projects were to incorporate objectives related to organizational performance, then the evaluation of these projects would begin to take this into account as well.

The World Bank has reported that in the past, agencies have too often focused on how much money they disbursed and on narrow physical implementation measures of the "success" of the projects that they financed. It turns out that neither measure tells much about the effectiveness of assistance. The evaluation of development aid should focus instead on the extent to which financial resources have contributed to sound policy environments. It should focus on whether agencies have used their resources to stimulate the policy reforms and institutional changes that lead to better outcomes.

Organizational Life Cycles and Performance Change

Successful implementation of an organizational assessment requires a good understanding of the stage of development within which the organization finds itself. Organizations are quite diverse as social units: they come in many sizes, shapes and variations. Some organizations are old, others young. A young organization in a growth stage needs different types of support than a mature organization that is relatively stable. Similarly, organizations with an uncertain mandate are of a different nature than those whose mandates are clear. Organizational variations play a big role in understanding how to interpret the information from an organizational assessment.

Organizations also emerge in any number of ways and are strongly influenced by their leadership. There are new leaders with a mandate for change; departing leaders who want to influence the future; and even departing leaders who perhaps want to avoid having evidence of performance come to light.

As organizations are constantly evolving, there can be difficulties in creating ways to understand the mix of performance areas. Do young organizations pay more attention to their effectiveness and financial stability? Is this normal? Should this be encouraged in an organizational assessment? Do mature organizations pay more attention to efficiency concerns? Relevance? How does the organizational life cycle affect the organizational assessment process?

The only certainty, unfortunately, would appear to be that there is no certain answer to any of these questions. As Aldrich (1999, p. 1) has written:

> I have been disappointed that most research on organizations focuses on structure and stability rather than emergence and change. By ignoring the question of origins, researchers have also avoided the question of why things persist. In contrast, the evolutionary approach to organizations treats origins and persistence as inseparable issues. In doing so, evolutionary models encompass many levels and units of analysis and thus typically take an interdisciplinary perspective.

Like many involved in the assessment process, Aldrich is intrigued by the complexity of organizations. Why do some organizations do well and others constantly fail? How does one identify the cluster of variables that can produce change? Why is it that some organizations resist change? We basically know that organizational change or stability is inextricably linked to time-dependent historical processes. Since organizational assessments take place at a given moment, it is important to contextualize the assessment. Has leadership just changed or not? Is the economic or social environment in turmoil? Is the organization attempting to renew itself, or engaging in a new mission?

The point is that the hypotheses or assumptions about what affects organizational performance are often mitigated by the organizational life cycle. While life cycle analysis is included in our framework, it is often necessary to rethink the effects of life cycle changes when making conclusions or hypotheses about change, since employees would then have nothing else in their lives.

We know that many events occur simultaneously, rather than sequentially, in an organization's life. Distinct capacities, motivation and environmental components may be separated out for analytical purposes, but in practice, they are linked in continuous feedback loops and cycles. So an assessment is really a snapshot of the organization at a given moment, using the analytical tools available. In this way, the assessment reflects the historical path of the organization's accumulated actions to date.

Does this change the organizational assessment? Does it affect how issues are framed? Is it reasonable to assume that there is a process dip? How does this affect the implementation process? Do aid projects exacerbate the situation? These are questions that must constantly be posed when assessing an organization's performance.

ENSURING STAFF INPUT

The decision by a research center in South Asia to undertake a self-assessment was strongly influenced by the director. He was to leave at the end of his mandate. Although his tenure had been successful, he foresaw some changes ahead that would affect the organization. He knew that the organization would have to adjust to address those changes, and he initiated the self-assessment to ensure that the staff would have input into that process when the new director arrived. During orientation visits prior to taking up his post, the new director was also involved in the design of the self-assessment. He, too, saw the value of staff input for improving performance. He also saw the benefits of such an assessment for the start-up of his directorship. In the end, the assessment was expanded to include the board as well.

Logic Models and Organizational Assessments

Organizations are goal-oriented systems driven by the actions of many people. Their actions are not random events, but rather are driven by the assumptions held by these individuals. These mental models are known as managerial cognition (Schein, 1997), or perceived organizational culture. They are cultural patterns that translate a world that is often ambiguous and complex into a more understandable and familiar system that fits the needs and expectations of the organization, and in which the organization can take logical decisions.

The organizational assessment model presented in this text is a diagnostic tool aimed at helping development workers better understand the performance of an organization, and assess the various components that might affect that performance in the future. It is a framework that absorbs complexity and provides a way to organize the ambiguous, uncertain world of organizations. It is also a way to get people to learn and think. The diagnosis of an organization should lead to ways to change organizational performance.

Today, logic models as seen in logical frameworks are used to help development agencies and international financial institutions describe the project interventions they will make in organizations. Logic systems help to clarify the performance requirements and the resources needed to affect project performance. Of interest to our work is that many times, the organizational assessment must link its findings to a logic model or logical framework. Can it? After all, projects are short term, while change in organizational performance is long term.

Projects are driven by a logic that is relatively linear: inputs lead to activities, which leads to outputs, which leads to outcomes, which leads to impacts. While this logic is useful for more focused activities, rarely does organizational change occur in this linear pattern. Rather, change in organizational performance is better depicted as a set of interactive or clustered changes that are perceived by organizational members in different ways and in different time dimensions.

Can we link our organizational assessment work with that of the logic models? Our experience indicates both yes and no. On the positive or yes side of the equation, we found it useful to create logical linkages between areas of diagnosed change and our performance model. For example, there is an assumed link between training community health workers in clinics and improving the performance of those clinics. The logic is that improving individual capability affects organizational performance. However, we know that there are many other conditions that must be considered as well.

Most of the conditions for success in terms of capacity and the environment can be identified or subsumed within a logical framework system. However, we often do not have the tools to understand or depict the complexity of dealing with organizational and member motivation. How do we get ownership for change? What are the ways we need to change norms and values? Thus, while we have found the logic systems to be helpful in depicting some of the capacity and environmental aspects that lead to organizational change, we have been less successful in using the logic systems to help us understand organizational motivation and the dynamics of change. This is an area that requires work.

CHANGING ORGANIZATIONAL FORMS

This framework was developed with the standard organization in mind. It is focused on the performance of an organization with the standard attributes of a board of some sort, and a director who is responsible as the leader to take decisions such as hiring staff to carry out functions, etc. The organization has a defined functional purpose. For example, a Ministry of Health has a functional responsibility to make sure that clean water is available.

Increasingly, activities are not carried out by a single organization. More and more organizations are realizing that many of the tasks that need to be carried out require collaboration with other types of organizations, such as networks, consortia and public-private partnerships. These have characteristics that are different from those of single organizations. The newer organizations are an amalgam of different functional types. Decisions are not taken in one location, but rather are spread according to function, responsibility and need. Therefore, when we try to implement our framework, it may or may not make sense to the organization because of its structure.

While there are many different forms of collaboration, they share some common characteristics. In a single organization, there is a clear domain of operation for the organization. It provides a particular kind of service to a certain group of clients. A collaboration tries to meet a need that is not always clearly defined and that is changing over time. Therefore, it is not always precisely clear what the partnership is doing, nor who within the partnership is doing what. Partnerships are frequently not as structured as organizations; they may or may not have a legal existence. Frequently, they are built around shared interests and business relationships. But whether or not they have a legal existence, they are not clearly owned by one individual or one organization. Ownership is spread across the group that is participating, and the parts maintain their allegiance so long as they feel a sense of ownership and that the partnership is meeting a perceived need.

While many organizations are set up as permanent entities, partnerships are not always intended to last indefinitely. They can be set up to deal with a very specific problem, and once that problem is dealt with (or changes), the partnership dissolves and new partnerships emerge around new problems.

All of these factors have implications for diagnosis of the performance of the partnership. We are only beginning to explore the use of the framework with these types of organizations. What remains to be explored is whether the differences are primarily in definition of what performance means, or if there are some different elements that are fundamental to the framework to enhance its applicability to the assessment of partnerships.

In the organizations with which we have dealt we know who is a member and who is not. In newer organizations, there are part-timers, volunteers, temporary help and permanent-partial employees, all of whom see themselves as part of the organization. Because these members may have multiple loyalties and multiple boundaries, the boundaries themselves are somewhat fuzzy.

What experience to date tells us is that the factors noted above call for a very different consideration of the structure of performance and its assessment. Because the boundaries are fuzzy, performance assessment that is concerned with efficiency is problematic: so long as the boundaries are not clear, it is hard to determine whose efficiency to assess, and in what terms. The lack of clarity in ownership is combined with the central importance of ownership in sustaining effective partnerships. This means that relevance must be very carefully defined, both from the perspective of the problem (or problematic), and from the perspective of each of the partners.

LIFE CYCLES OF PARTNERSHIPS

The variable permanence of partnerships suggests that their life cycles are quite different from those of individual organizations. They may fold at what seems the peak of success, precisely because the issue they were dealing with has been addressed. Looking at partnerships and coalitions from this perspective may provide many clues as to the rise and fall of NGOs. In some cases, the decline of a partnership may be a cause for celebration of its successful performance.

Conclusions

Universalia has worked for almost six years with the Inter-American Development Bank and the International Development Research Centre to promote dialogue in order to improve organizational assessment. This book is the latest in that series. It is an update of our original book in 1995, with various portions reframed. The sections on performance and capacity have been rewritten based on our experience during this period, together with other agencies that have graciously shared their experiences and analysis with us.

Other organizations, such the World Conservation Union and the International Service for National Agricultural Research, are attempting to use the framework within their own organizational spheres. Many individuals and organizations have used the framework and have shared their experiences with us. The effort to help organizations improve their performance is ongoing. There are no cut-and-dried answers to the various problems encountered while conducting organizational assessments in less developed countries.

ENVIRONMENT ASSESSMENT QUESTIONS

Formal Rules

Administrative/Legal Environment
How is the organization affected by the administrative and legal environment?

Administrative

- Has the organization identified other institutions/organizations/groups to which it relates or might be expected to relate?
- Has the organization been identified as influential or important to the sector by consumers, policymakers, suppliers, competitors and other organizations in its external environment?
- Are the organization's objectives complementary to those of other organizations?
- Do the norms and values of the organization support the work that it intends to carry out?
- Are there useful (formal and informal) conflict resolution systems?
- Is the organization affected by bureaucracy (red tape)?

Legal

- Has the organization clearly defined the role played by its legal framework?
- Does the legal framework support the organization's autonomy?
- Is the organization's legal framework clear?
- Is the legal framework consistent with current practice?
- Is the legal regulatory context conducive to work?
- Is relevant legislation up to date?
- Is the judicial system responsive?
- Is the organization affected by:
    - Labor legislation?
    - A regulatory framework?
    - Environmental laws?
    - A public service commission?
    - Public sector reform?
    - Global and regional agreements and standards?

Political Environment

How is the organization affected by the political environment?

- Do government political and ideological trends support the organization's type of work?
- Does the government system facilitate collaborative arrangements?
- Does the organization have a role to play in national or sector development?
- How motivated is the organization to play its role in national or sector development?
- Does the organization have access to government funding?
- Does the organization have access to international funding?
- Does the organization have access to government knowledge and publications?
- Are there government policies and programs supporting the organization?
- What form of government is involved in the organization's internal affairs?
- What is the government's level of involvement in the organization's internal affairs?
- What effect do international relations have on the organization?
- How much does the government allow civil society to participate in its decision-making process?
- What is the level of political stability?
- How tolerant is the government of risk and the ability to manage change?
- How do political groups pressure the government to affect policy and priorities?
- How much is the organization affected by political corruption, violence or strikes?
- How responsive is the government system to the organization's needs and issues?

Economic Environment

How is the organization affected by the economic environment?

- Does economic policy support the organization's ability to acquire technologies and financial resources?
- Is money available to do work?
- Do donors give their support?
- Is the budget allocation adequate for the organization's work?
- Is external financing available?
- Are there supportive monetary and fiscal policies (including interest rates)?
- Is the debt burden restrictive?
- Are emerging markets conducive?

- Is the currency stable?
- Is there a competitive market environment?
- Are policies and programs threatened by the informal sector?
- Is the economic growth rate supportive of development?
- Is the public service investment program reflective of government priorities?
- Is the tax policy regressive?
- What is the industrial relations climate?
- Are employment rates acceptable?
- Are trade agreements supportive of the country's comparative advantage (globalization and free market)?
- What effect is globalization having on the economy?
- What effect is globalization having on the organization?
- Are input costs restrictive?
- Is the financial sector conducive to economic development?

INSTITUTIONAL ETHOS

Social and Cultural Environment

How is the organization affected by the social and cultural environment?

- Does the organization support equity in the workplace?
- Does the organization account for the effect of culture on program complexity?
- Do prevailing social and cultural values support the organization's work?
- Does the organization have access to a pool of capable human resources from which it can recruit staff?
- Is the organization affected by:
    - Religious/ethnic/gender/class customs and biases?
    - Cultural values/norms (e.g., Christmas holidays)?
    - Violence and crime?
    - Security issues on project sites?
    - Nepotism?
    - Corruption?
    - Chronic diseases, health, nutrition (can be a whole new category)?
    - Cultural behavior?
    - Preconceived attitudes toward donor agencies?
    - Political/social instability (e.g., mafias)?

CAPABILITIES

Technology Environment

Is the technology needed to carry out the organization's work supported by systems in the broader environment?

- Is there adequate physical infrastructure (power, telecommunication, transport) to support the organization's work?
- Is the technology needed by the organization to carry out its work supported by the overall level of national technological development?
- Does the system of government facilitate the organization's process of acquiring needed technology?
- Is human resource development adequate to support new technology?
- How reliable are available utilities, particularly electric power?
- How stable is the cost of available utilities?
- Are trainer resources available?
- What is the organization's networking capability?
- How adequate are the organization's data processing facilities?
- Does the organization have access to research?

Ecological and Geographical Environment

- Will the organization's services be affected by natural phenomena?
- Are the natural environmental conditions conducive and supportive of the organization's work, or do they impose additional costs or technical challenges?
- Does pollution affect the pace of the organization's work?
- How will environmental and natural resources policy and legislation affect the organization's performance?

REMEMBER:

A checklist is a useful tool, but it is only a starting point that needs to be continuously renewed and revised.

AN ORGANIZATIONAL
ASSESSMENT

SAMPLE REPORT OUTLINE

1. Introduction
- Background and purpose
- Development issues
- Description of the organization
- Unit of analysis

2. Methodology
- Major issues/questions
- Data collection/sources
- Data analysis
- Limitations (time, resources, information)
- Team
- Schedule

3. Targeting Individual Organization or Network
- Identification of organization
- Profile of organization
- Organizational links to development problem

4. Enabling Environment
Formal rules
- Legal framework
- Intellectual property rights
- Mandate
- Labor rights

Institutional ethos
- History
- Cultural values
- Norms
- Taboos

Capabilities
- Natural resources
- Human resources
- Technology
- Financial resources

5. Major Organizational Capacity Issues Affecting Organizational Performance
- Strategic leadership
- Structure
- Human resources
- Finance
- Program/services
- Infrastructure
- Technology
- Inter-organizational linkages

6. Major Organizational Motivation Issues Affecting Organizational Performance
- Mission
- Vision
- History
- Culture
- System of incentives and rewards

7. Organizational Performance
- Effectiveness
- Efficiency
- Ongoing relevance
- Financial viability

8. Conclusions and Recommendations
- Areas for further study
- Possible areas for intervention
- Possible ways of implementing the project

Glossary

Term	Definition
Assessment	Often used as a synonym for evaluation; sometimes recommended for approaches that report measurement without making judgments on the measurements.
Assumptions	The external factors, influences, situations or conditions that are necessary for project success. Assumptions are external factors that are quite likely but not certain to occur and which are important for the success of the project or program, but which are largely or completely beyond the control of project management.
Audit	An examination or review that assesses and reports on the extent to which a condition, process or performance conforms to predetermined standards or criteria.
Baseline/ Baseline data	The set of conditions existing at the outset of a program. Periodic comparisons to the baseline state can determine progress, or lack thereof.
Benchmark	A reference point or standard against which progress or achievements may be compared.
Benchmarking	Compares that which is being measured to a benchmark such as best practices in the field, including professional or scientific standards.
Bias	The extent to which a measurement or method systematically underestimates or overestimates a value.

Capabilities	Resources within a society that influence the type and scale of activity undertaken by individuals and organizations (e.g., natural resources, infrastructure, human resources, technology).
Capacity	Organizational and technical abilities, relationships and values that enable countries, organizations, groups and individuals at any level to carry out functions and achieve their development objectives over time.
Capacity building	The ability of individuals, groups, institutions and organizations to identify and solve development problems over time.
Capacity development	The process by which individuals, organizations, institutions and societies develop their individual and collective abilities to perform functions, solve problems and set and achieve objectives.
Case	The phenomenon to be investigated in case study research. The term is also used for clinical "cases" such as the behavior pattern of an individual.
Case study	A research process focused on understanding a specific phenomenon, within its real life context, generally involving multiple sources of information.
Ceremonial assessments	Refers to the control of data to a few offices and individuals during an assessment of organizational performance with the intent of carefully hiding any criticism directed at the organization in question.
Client	The person, group or agency that has commissioned an evaluation and to whom the evaluator has legal responsibility.

Conclusion

A reasoned judgment based on a synthesis of findings.

Conflict of interest

When there is a clash between the private interest and the public interest of a person responsible for an evaluation. It is not necessarily fatal to validity (e.g., self-evaluation is a legitimate strategy), but may affect credibility unless various interests are suitably balanced.

Culture

Set of values, guiding beliefs, understandings and ways of thinking that are shared by members of an organization and are taught to new members. Culture represents the unwritten, informal standards of an organization.

Dependent variable

A variable that is thought to be affected or influenced by a program.

Effectiveness

The extent to which objectives or planned outputs have been achieved.

Empowerment evaluation

Empowers those involved in an evaluation study by giving them new knowledge of their performance. Enabling environment.

Enabling environment

Attitudes, policies and practices that stimulate and support effective and efficient functioning of organizations and individuals.

Evaluability

The extent to which a project or program has been defined in such a way as to enable subsequent evaluation.

Financial viability

An organization's ability to maintain the inflow of financial resources greater than the outflow.

Finding

A factual statement about the program based on evidence. It may involve a synthesis of data and, therefore, judgment.

Focus group	A carefully planned and moderated informal discussion where one person's ideas bounce off those of another, creating a chain reaction of informative dialogue. The purpose is to address a specific topic in depth and in a comfortable environment in order to elicit a wide range of opinions, attitudes, feelings and perceptions from a group of individuals who share some common experience relative to the dimension under study.
Governance	Issues and problems involved in aligning the interests of those who manage an organization with those who are responsible for its results, who own it, and with outsiders who have a stake in the organization.
Impact	The ultimate planned and unplanned consequences of a program; an expression of the changes actually produced as a result of the program, typically several years after the program has stabilized or been completed.
Indicator	An explicit measure used to determine performance; a signal that reveals progress towards objectives; a means of measuring what actually happens against what has been planned in terms of quality, quantity and timeliness.
Infrastructure	Reference to the basic conditions (facilities and technology) that allow work to go on within the organization (e.g., adequate lighting, clean water).
Input	Resources that are required for achieving the stated results by producing the intended outputs through relevant activities (e.g., human resources, materials, services).
Institutional ethos	Implicit or unwritten codes that include cultural values, norms, religious precepts and taboos. Also known as "informal rules of the game."

Leadership	Process whereby an individual engages in processes of influencing a group of individuals to achieve a common purpose.
Likert scale	A scale that asks respondents to indicate the extent to which they agree or disagree with a statement. Five and seven point scales are the most common; three can be used for special situations and children.
Logic models	The translation of assumptions and mental models of individuals into understandable and familiar systems that complement the needs and expectations of an organization, thus allowing it to make logical decisions.
Missing data	Data that the evaluator intended to collect but was unable to for a variety reasons (e.g., the inability to interview a key informant, limited access to a research setting, blank items on a questionnaire, data entry errors).
Monitoring	An ongoing process to verify systematically that planned activities or processes take place as expected or that progress is being made in achieving planned outputs.
Motivation	An intrinsic and moral desire to achieve a purpose.
Niche management	Type of management that involves the identification of and concentration on a competitively valuable capability (or set of capabilities) that an organization has more of or can do better than its rivals.
Objective	Expresses a particular effect that the program is expected to achieve if completed successfully according to plan.
Ongoing relevance	Ability of an organization to meet the needs and gain the support of its priority stakeholders in the past, present and future.

Opportunity cost   The value that one gives up by selecting one of several mutually exclusive alternatives.

Outcome   An effect or consequence of a program in the medium term. Between an output that is short term and one that is often considered to be five years or more from the program intervention. A medium-term result that is the logical consequence of achieving a combination of outputs.

Output   The physical products, institutional and operational changes, or improved skills and knowledge to be achieved by the project or program as a result of good management of inputs and activities. The immediate, visible, concrete and tangible consequences of project inputs.

Primary data   Information obtained first-hand by the researcher.

Program   A group of related projects, services and activities directed to the achievement of specific goals.

Program evaluation   The process of making judgments about a program based on information and analysis relative to such issues as relevance, cost-effectiveness and success for its stakeholders.

Program rationale   The fundamental reason(s) why a program exists, together with its underlying assumptions.

Project   A planned undertaking designed to achieve certain specific objectives within a given budget and a specified period of time.

Project trap   A situation in which a project takes precedence over an organization and its mission, possibly leading to organizational decline.

Qualitative data	Data that use non-numeric information for description. Generally words, but may include photographs and films, audio recordings, and artifacts.
Quantitative data	Information that describes, explains and reports on phenomena using numbers.
Questionnaire	A set of written questions used to collect data from respondents.
Relevance	The degree to which the purpose of a project or program remains valid and pertinent.
Reliability	The quality of a measurement process that would produce similar results from (1) repeated observations of the same condition or event, or from (2) multiple observations of the same condition or event by different means. Reliability also refers to the extent that a data collection instrument will yield the same results each time it is administered. In qualitative research, reliability refers to the extent that different researchers, given exposure to the same situation, would reach the same conclusions.
Result	Describable or measurable change in a given state that is derived from a cause-and-effect relationship.
Return on investment	In fiscal evaluation, the ratio of benefits to costs, generally expressed as a percentage.
Rules	Legal or regulatory structures within an organization. Rules are one of the most important ingredients of an enabling environment.
Sample	A subset of a population.

Stakeholders　　　Any group within or outside an organization that has a stake in the organization's performance. Creditors, suppliers, employees and owners are all stakeholders.

Success　　　A favorable program or project result that is assessed in terms of such considerations as effectiveness, impact, sustainability and contributions to capacity development.

Terms of reference　　　The focus and boundaries of a contract research project, including a statement about who the research is for, the research objective, major issues and questions, and sometimes the schedule and available resources.

Triangulation　　　A process of using multiple data sources, data collection methods, and/or theories to validate research findings, help eliminate bias, and detect errors or anomalies in discoveries.

Unit of analysis　　　The actual object being investigated (e.g., persons, classrooms, organizations, nations).

Validity　　　The largest methodological challenge to organizational assessment, validity refers to the ability of a methodology to be relevant and meaningful as well as appropriate to an organization's mission.

Validity of an evaluation　　　The extent to which an evaluation's conclusions are justified by the data presented.

Variable　　　A characteristic that can assume any one of a range of values.

Work plan　　　A document that details the resources and methodology to be used in conducting an evaluation.

Bibliography

Aldrich, H. 1999. *Organizations Evolving*. London, Thousand Oaks, CA.: Sage.

Allcorn, S. 1995. Understanding Organizational Culture and the Quality of Workplace Subjectivity. *Human Relations* 48(1): 73-96.

Allen, R. 1995. On a Clear Day You Can Have a Vision: A Visioning Model for Everyone. *Leadership and Organizational Development Journal* 16(4): 39-44.

Anderson, G. 1998. *Fundamentals of Educational Research*. Second edition. London: Falmer.

Anderson, G., and D. Gilsig. 1998. Participatory Evaluation in Human Resource Development: A Case Study from Southeast Asia. In Ted Jackson and Yusuf Kassam (eds.), *Knowledge Shared: Participatory Evaluation in Development: Cooperation*. Ottawa: IDRC and Kumarian Press.

Bajaj, M. 1997. *Revisiting Evaluation: A Study of the Process, Role and Contribution of Donor Funded Evaluations to Development Organizations in South Asia*. Ottawa: IDRC.

Barker, R.C. 1995. Financial Performance Measurement: Not a Total Solution. *Management Decision* 33(2): 31-39.

Baron, A. 1995. Project Highlights Culture Change in Public Sector. *Personnel Management* 1(7): 60.

Bart, C. 1997. Sex, Lies and Mission Statements. *Business Horizons* (November/December): 9-18.

Bate, P. 1996. *Strategies for Cultural Change*. New York: Butterworth-Heinemann.

Bates, R., and A. Krueger (eds.). 1993. *Political and Economic Interactions in Economic Policy Reform*. Oxford, UK: Blackwell.

Beaton, G. 1994. Mission Statements in Professional Service Firms: Direction or Decoration? *Journal of Professional Services Marketing* 11(1): 173-88.

Beesley, A. 1995. "Time Compression" - New Source of Competitiveness in the Supply-Chain. *Logistics Focus* (5): 24-25.

Bennett, R. 1993. Developing People for Real: Some Issues and Approaches. *Management Decision* 31(3): 55-61.

Bennis, W. 1969. *Organization Development: Its Nature, Origins and Prospects*. Reading, MA.: Addison-Wesley.

Bennis, W., and J. Goldsmith. 1997. *Learning to Lead: A Workbook on Becoming a Leader*. Cambridge, MA: Perseus Press.

Berry, A. J., P. Capps, D. Cooper, and P. Fergusson. 1985. Management Control in the Area of the NCB. *Accounting, Organizations and Society* (1): 3-28.

Birkin, F., and D. Woodward. 1997. Management Accounting for Sustainable Development. *Management Accounting* (July/ August): 42-45.

Blau, P., and R. Scott. 1962. *Formal Organizations*. San Francisco: Chandler Publishing.

Blickendorfer, R., and J. Janey. 1988. Measuring Performance in Nonprofit Organizations (Part 2). *Nonprofit World* 6(2): 18-22.

Bloor, G., and P. Dawson. 1994. Understanding Professional Culture in Organizational Context. *Organization Studies* 15(2): 275-95.

Booth, R. 1996. Accountants Do It by Proxy. *Management Accounting-London* 74(5): 48.

———. 1998. Program Management: Measures for Program Action. *Management Accounting—London* 76(7): 26-28.

Boschken, H. L. 1994. Organizational Performance and Multiple Constituencies. *Public Administration Review* 54: 308-12.

Bowles, M. L., and G. Coates. 1993. Image and Substance: The Management of Performance as Rhetoric or Reality? *Personnel Review* 22(2): 3-21.

Brown, M. G. 1994. Is Your Measurement System Well Balanced? *Journal for Quality and Participation* 17(6): 6-11.

Brown, S. J., and R.J. Kraft. 1998. A Strategy for the Emerging HR Role. *Human Resources Professional* 11(2): 28-32.

Brudney, J., and S. Condrey. 1993. Pay for Performance: Explaining the Differences in Managerial Motivation. *Public Productivity and Management Review* 17(2): 129-44.

Burki, S., and G.E. Perry. 1998. *Beyond the Washington Consensus: Institutions Matter*. Washington, D.C.: World Bank.

Byrd, R. E. 1987. Corporate Leadership Skills: A Synthesis. *Organizational Dynamics* 16(1): 34-43.

Calfee, D. 1993. Get Your Mission Statement Working. *Management Review* (January): 54-57.

Campbell, J.P., et al. 1970. *Managerial Behavior, Performance and Effectiveness*. New York: McGraw-Hill.

Campbell, D.T., and J.C. Stanley. 1963. *Experimental and Quasi-experimental Designs for Research*. Chicago: Rand McNally.

Canadian Comprehensive Auditing Foundation (CCAF). 1996. *Accountability, Performance Reporting, Comprehensive Audit: An Integrated Perspective*. Ottawa: CCAF.

Caplow, T. 1976. *How to Run Any Organization: A Manual of Practical Sociology*. Hinsdale, IL: The Dryden Press.

Carver, J. 1996. *Basic Principle of Policy Governance*. San Francisco: Jossey-Bass.

Chelimsky, E. 1997. The Coming Transformations in Evaluation. In E. Chelimsky and W.R. Shadish (eds.), *Evaluation for the 21st Century: A Handbook*. Thousand Oaks, CA.: Sage.

Chhibber, A. 1998. Institutions, Policies and Development Outcomes. In R. Picciotto and E. Weisner (eds.), *Evaluation and Development: The Institutional Dimension*. Washington, D.C.: World Bank.

Chilton, K. 1994. *The Global Challenge of American Manufacturer*. St. Louis: Washington University.

Chong, A., and C. Claderon. 1997. *Institutional Change and Poverty, or Why it is Worth it to Reform the State*. Washington, D.C.: World Bank.

Clague, C., P. Keefer, S. Knack, and M. Olson. 1997. Institutions and Economic Performance: Property Rights and Contract Enforcement. In C. Clague (ed.), *Institutions and Economic Development: Growth and Governance in Less-Developed and Post-Socialist Countries*.

Cockerill, T., J. Hunt, and H. Schroder. 1995. Managerial Competencies: Fact or Fiction? *Business Strategy Review* 6: 1-12.

Cohen, S. A. 1993. Defining and Measuring Effectiveness in Public Management. *Public Productivity and Management Review* 17(1): 45-57.

Colvard, J. E. 1994. In Defense of Middle Management. *Government Executive* 26(5): 57-58.

Coyne, K., and R. Dye. 1998. The Competitive Dynamics of Network-Based Businesses. *Harvard Business Review* (January-February): 99-109.

Datta, S. K., and J.B. Nugent. 1998. Transaction Cost Economics and Contractual Choice: Theory and Evidence. In M. Nabli and J. B. Nugent (eds.), *The Institutional Economics and Development*. Amsterdam: Elsevier Science Publishers.

Deming, W.E. 1986. *Out of the Crisis*. Cambridge, MA.: MIT Press.

Denison, D. 1996. What Is the Difference between Organizational Culture and Organizational Climate? *Academy of Management Review* 21(3): 619-54.

Dent, S. M., and P.A. Hughes. 1998. Core Process Management: Getting Everyone on the Same Page. *Journal of Quality and Participation* 21(6): 50-55.

Desormeaux, G. 1998. Institutional Structure and Social Security Systems: Lessons from the Chilean Experience. In R. Picciotto and E. Weisner (eds.), *Evaluation and Development: The Institutional Dimension*. Washington, D.C.: World Bank.

Down, J. W., W. Mardis, T.R. Connolly, and S. Johnson. 1997. A Strategic Model Emerges. HR *Focus* 74(6): 22-23.

Drucker, P. F. 1983. *The Concept of the Corporation*. New York: New American Library.

Dunn, W.N. 1982. Reforms as Arguments. *Knowledge: Creation, Diffusion, Utilization* 3(3): 293-326.

Earl, S., F. Carden, and T. Smutylo. 2001. *Outcome Mapping: Building Learning and Reflection into Development Programs*. Ottawa: International Development Research Centre.

Eaton, J. 1972. *Institution Building and Development: From Concepts to Complications* Beverly Hills, CA.: Sage.

Eggertsson, T. 1996. A Note on the Economics of Institutions. In A. Alston and T. Eggertsson (eds.), *Empirical Studies in Institutional Change*. Cambridge, UK: Cambridge University Press.

Eimicke, W. B. 1998. Benchmarking for Best Practices in the Public Sector/Achieving Improved Performances in Public Organizations: A Guide for Managers/ Organizational Performance and Measurement in the Public Sector: Toward Service, Effort and Accomplishment Reported. *American Review of Public Administration* 28(1): 90-95.

Engerman, S. L. 1997. Cultural Values, Ideological Beliefs, and Changing Labor Institutions: Notes on their Interactions. In J. Drobak and J. V. C. Nye (eds.), *The Frontiers of the New International Economics*. San Diego: Academic Press Limited.

Ensminger, J. 1997. Changing Property Rights: Reconciling Formal and Informal Rights to Land in Africa. In J. Drobak and J. V. C. Nye (eds.), *The Frontiers of the New Institutional Economics*. San Diego: Academic Press Limited.

Eriksson, J. 1998. An Institutional Framework for Learning from Failed States. In R. Picciotto and E. Weisner (eds.), *Evaluation and Development: The Institutional Dimension*. Washington, D.C.: World Bank.

Etzioni, A. 1964. *Modern Organizations*. Englewood Cliff, CA.: Prentice Hall.

Fetterman, D.M., S. Kaftarian, and A. Wandersman. 1996. *Empowerment Evaluation: Knowledge and Tools for Self-assessment and Accountability*. Thousand Oaks, CA: Sage.

Gagnon, Y., and J. Dragon. 1996. The Impact of Technology on Organizational Performance. *Optimum, The Journal of Public Sector Management* 28(1): 19-31.

Galbraith, J. 1973. *Designing Complex Organizations*. Reading, MA.: Addison-Wesley.

Georgopoulos, B., and A. Tannenbaum. 1957. A Study of Organizational Effectiveness. *American Sociological Review* 22: 534-40.

Gerhart, B., and G.T. Milkovich. 1990. Organizational Differences in Managerial Compensation and Financial Performance. *Academy of Management Journal* 33(4): 663-91.

Goddard, A., and J. Powell. 1994. *Accountability and Accounting. Accounting, Auditing and Accountability Journal* 7(2): 50-69.

Graf, L., M. Hemmasi, and K.C. Strong. 1996. Strategic Analysis for Resource Allocation Decisions in Health Care Organizations. *Journal of Managerial Issues* 8(1): 92-107.

Grandori, A. 1997. An Organizational Assessment of Interfirm Coordination Modes. *Organization Studies* 18(6): 897-925.

Greenhill, R. 1995. State Intervention in the Brazilian Coffee Trade During the 1920's: A Case Study of New Institutional Economics. In J. Hariss, J. Turner and C. M. Lewis (eds.), *The New Institutional Economics and Third World Development*. New York: Routledge.

Guba, E.G., and Y.S. Lincoln. 1989. *Fourth Generation Evaluation*. Newbury Park, CA: Sage.

Gupta, N., and D. Jenkins. 1996. The Politics of Pay. *Compensation and Benefits Review* (March/April): 23-30.

Gupta, Y. P., and D. Chin. 1994. Organizational Life Cycles: A Review and Proposed Directions for Research. *The Mid-Atlantic Journal of Business* 30(3): 269-93.

Hagen, A. F., M. T. Hassan, and S.G. Amin. 1998. Critical Strategic Leadership Components: An Empirical Investigation. SAM *Advanced Management Journal* 63(3): 39-44.

Haggard, S., and R. Kaufman (eds.). 1992. *The Politics of Economic Adjustment.* Princeton, NJ: Princeton University Press.

Hahm, Hongjoo. 1993. *The Development of the Private Sector in a Small Economy in Transition.* World Bank Discussion Papers, East Asia and Pacific Region Series, 223. World Bank, Washington D.C.

Haire, M. 1956. *Psychology in Management.* New York: McGraw-Hill.

Handa, V., and A. Adas. 1996. Predicting the Level of Organizational Effectiveness: A Methodology for the Construction Firm. *Construction Management and Economics* 14(4): 341-352.

Handy, C. 1997. Managing the Dream. *Executive Excellence* 14(11): 11-12.

Harrison, M. I. 1987. *Diagnosing Organizations: Methods, Models and Processes.* Beverly Hills, CA.: Sage.

Harrison, R. 1997. Why Your Firm Needs Emotional Intelligence. *People Management* (1): 41.

Hassard, J., and M. Parker (eds.). 1993. *Post Modernism and Organizations.* London: Sage.

Hatch, M. J. 1993. The Dynamics of Organizational Culture. *Academy of Management Review* 18(4): 657-93.

Healthcare Financial Management. 1997. Key Organizational Performance Indicators. *Healthcare Financial Management* 51(4).

Heckman, J., C. Heinrich, and J. Smith. 1997. Assessing the Performance of Performance Standards in Public Bureaucracies. *American Economic Review* 87(2): 389-95.

Henke, E. O. 1992. Use of Accounting Data by Externally Interested Parties. In E. O. Henke (ed.), *Introduction to Nonprofit Organization Accounting.* Cincinnati: South-Western Publishing Company.

Hesselbein, F., M. Goldsmith, and R. Beckhard. 1996. *The Organization of the Future.* San Francisco: Jossey-Bass.

Hickson, D., and D. Pugh. 1995. *Management Worldwide: The Impact of Societal Culture on Organizations around the Globe.* London: Penguin Books.

Howard, R. 1990. Values Make the Company. *Harvard Business Review* 68(5): 133-44.

Hunter, J. D., and C.M. Lewis (eds.). 1997. *The New Institutional Economics of the Third World.* London: Routledge.

Inter-American Development Bank.1997. *Evaluation: A Management Tool for Improving Project Performance*. IDB, Washington, D.C.

————. 1999. Annual Report on Projects in Execution. Document CP-199, May 26.

International Development Research Centre (IDRC). 1987. *Approaches to Strengthening Research Institutions*. Ottawa: IDRC.

Israel, A. 1990. *The Changing Role of the State: Institutional Dimensions*. World Bank Working Paper Series 495 (August). World Bank, Washington, D.C.

Kaji, G. 1998. Institutions in Development: the Country, Research, and Operational Challenges. In R. Picciotto and E. Weisner (eds.), *Evaluation and Development: The Institutional Dimension*. World Bank, Washington, D.C.

Kaplan, R. S., and D.P. Norton. 1996. Using the Balanced Scorecard as a Strategic Management System. *Harvard Business Review* 74(1): 75-85.

Ketchen, D. J. J., J.B. Thomas, and R.R.J. McDaniel. 1996. Process, Content and Context: Synergistic Effects on Organizational Performance. *Journal of Management* 22(2): 231-57.

Khandker, S. R., B. Khalily, and Z. Khan. 1995. *Grameen Bank: Performance and Sustainability*. World Bank Discussion Paper No. 306, Washington, D.C.

Kilmann, R., and I. Kilmann. 1989. *Managing beyond the Quick Fix: A Completely Integrated Program for Creating and Maintaining Organizational Success*. San Francisco: Jossey-Bass.

Korey, G. 1995. TDM Grid: An Effective Tool for Implementing Strategic Plans in Academic Institutions. *Management Decision* 33(2): 40-47.

Kotter, J. P. 1990. What Leaders Really Do. *Harvard Business Review* 68(3): 103-11.

Lal, D. 1996. Participation, Markets and Democracy. In M. Lundahl and B. Ndulu (eds.), *New Directions in Development Economics: Growth, Environmental Concerns and Government in the 1990's*. New York: Routledge.

Lampe, J. C., and S.G. Sutton. 1997. Performance Measures to Improve Internal Audit Productivity and Quality. *Internal Auditing* 13(1): 3-14.

Lawrence, P. R., and J.W. Lorsch. 1967. *Organization and Environment*. Boston: Harvard University Press.

Levinson, H. 1972. *Organizational Diagnostics*. Cambridge, MA.: Harvard University Press.

Likert, R. 1957. *Some Applications of Behavioral Research*. Paris: UNESCO.

Lorenzoni, G., and C. Baden-Fuller. 1995. Creating a Strategic Center to Manage a Web of Partners. *California Management Review* 37(3): 146-63.

Love, A.J. 1991. *Internal Evaluation: Building Organizations from Within*. Newbury Park, CA.: Sage.

Lusthaus, C., M. Adrien, and M. Perstinger. 1999. *Capacity Building: Implications for Planning, Monitoring and Evaluation*. Montreal: Universalia.

Lusthaus, C., M. Adrien, G. Anderson, and F. Carden. 1999. *Enhancing Organizational Performance: A Toolbox for Self-assessment*. Ottawa: International Development Research Centre.

Lusthaus, C., G. Anderson, and M. Adrien. 1997. Organizational Self-Evaluation: An Emerging Frontier for Organizational Self-improvement. *Knowledge and Policy: The International Journal of Knowledge Transfer and Utilization* 10(1): 83-96.

Lusthaus, C., G. Anderson, M. Adrien and E. Murphy. 1996. *Evaluation institutionelle: Cadre pour le renforcement des organisations partenaires du CRDI*. Ottawa: CRDI.

Lusthaus, C., G. Anderson, and E. Murphy. 1995. *Institutional Assessment: A Framework for Strengthening Organizational Capacity for IDRC's Research Partners*. Ottawa: International Development Research Centre.

Manning, N. 2000. *Administration and Civil Service Assessment Tool*. Washington, D.C.: World Bank.

March, J. G., and R.I. Sutton. 1997. Organizational Performance as a Dependent Variable. *Organization Science* 8(6): 698-706.

Maslow, A. 1997. *Motivation and Personality*. New York: Harper and Row.

Mauro, P. 1995. Corruption and Growth. *Quarterly Journal of Economics* 110: 681-712.

McNerney, D. J. 1995. "Designer" Downsizing: Accent on Core Competencies. HR *Focus* 72(2).

Meyer, D. 1995. *Structural Cybernetics: An Overview*. Ridgefield, CT: N. Dean Meyer and Associates Inc.

Meyers, P., and I. Briggs. 1980. *Gifts Differing*. Palo Alto, CA.: Consulting Psychologist Press.

Mintzberg, H., and J.B. Quinn. 1995. *The Strategy Process: Concepts, Context and Cases*. New York: Prentice Hall.

Miron, D., S. Leichtman, and A. Atkins. 1993. Reengineering Human Resource Processes. *Human Resources Professional* 6(1): 19-23.

Morgan, P. 1998. *Capacity and Capacity Development - Some Strategies*. Hull: Policy Branch, CIDA.

Mueller, F. 1995. Organizational and Employee Cooperation: Can We Learn from Economists? *Human Relations* 48(10): 1217-235.

Nabli, M., and J.B. Nugent. 1989. Collective Action, Institutions and Development. In M. Nabli and J. B. Nugent (eds.), *The New Institutional Economics and Development*. Amsterdam: Elsevier Science Publishers.

Nanus, B. 1989. *The Leader's Edge*. Chicago: Contemporary Books.

North, D. 1990. *Institutions, Institutional Change and Economic Performance*. Cambridge, UK: Cambridge University Press.

North, D. C. 1994. Economic Performance through Time. *The American Economic Review* 84(3).

North, W.H. 1997. The Independent Evaluation of the Global Environment Facility Pilot Phase. In E. Chelimsky and W.R. Shadish (eds.), *Evaluation for the 21st century: A Handbook*. Thousand Oaks, CA: Sage.

Nourzad, F. 1997. *Infrastructure Capital and Private Sector Productivity: A Dynamic Analysis*. Milwaukee: Marquette University.

Nugent, J. B. 1998. Institutions, Markets and Outcomes. In R. Picciotto and E. Weisner (eds.), *Evaluation and Development: The Institutional Dimension*. Washington, D.C.: World Bank.

Nye, J. V. C. 1997. Thinking About the State: Property Rights, Trade and Changing Contractual Arrangements in a World with Coercion. In J. Drobak and J. V. C. Nye (eds.), *The Frontiers of the New Institutional Economics*. San Diego: Academic Press Limited.

Osborne, D., and T. Gaebler. 1992. *Reinventing Government: How the Entrepreneurial Spirit Is Transforming the Public Sector*. Reading, MA: Addison-Wesley.

Ostrom, E. 1997. Investing in Capital, Institutions and Incentives. In C. Clague (ed.), *Institutional and Economic Development: Growth and Governance in Less-Developed Post-Socialist Countries*. London: John Hopkins Press.

Ouchi, W. 1981. *Theory Z: How American Business Can Meet the Japanese Challenge*. Reading, MA: Addison-Wesley.

Patton, M.Q. 1990. *Qualitative Evaluation and Research Methods*. Second edition. Newbury Park, CA: Sage.

Peters, T. J., and R.H.J. Waterman. 1982. *In Search of Excellence*. New York: Warner Books.

———. 1988. *In Search of Excellence: Lessons from America's Best Run Companies*. New York: Warner Books.

Picciotto, R., and E. Weisner (eds.). 1998. *Evaluation and Development: The Institutional Dimension*. Wasington, D.C.: World Bank.

Quinn, R. E., and J. Rohrbaugh. 1983. A Spatial Model of Effectiveness Criteria: Towards a Competing Values Approach to Organizational Analysis. *Management Science* (29): 363-77.

Roethlisberger, F., and W. Dickson. 1939. *Management and the Worker*. Cambridge, MA: Harvard University Press.

Salopek, J. 1998. The New Managerial Mentor: Becoming a Learning Leader to Build Communities of Purpose. *Training and Development* 52(12): 61.

Savedoff, W. D. (ed.). 1998. *Organization Matters: Agency Problems in Health and Education in Latin America*. Washington, D.C.: Inter-American Development Bank.

Schein, E. 1997. *Organizational Culture and Leadership*. San Francisco: Jossey-Bass.

Schick, A. 1993. *A Performance-Based Budgeting System for the Agency for International Development*. Washington, D.C.: USAID.

Scott, R., and J. Meyer. 1994. *Institutional Environments and Organizations*. Thousand Oaks, CA: Sage.

Scott, W. R. 1995. *Institutions and Organizations*. Thousand Oaks, CA: Sage.

Scriven, M. 1991. *Evaluation Thesaurus*. Fourth edition. Thousand Oaks, CA: Sage.

———. 1997. Truth and Objectivity in Evaluation. In E. Chelimsky and W.R. Shadish (eds.), *Evaluation for the 21st Century: A Handbook*. Thousand Oaks, CA: Sage.

Selznick, P. 1957. *Leadership in Administration: A Sociological Interpretation*. Evanston, IL: Peterson Row.

Senge, P. M., C. Roberts, R.B. Ross, and B.J Smith. 1999. *The Dance of Change: The Challenges to Sustaining Momentum in Learning Organizations*. New York: Currency Doubleday.

Senge, P. M., C. Roberts, R.B. Ross, B.J. Smith, and A. Kleiner. 1994. *The Fifth Discipline Fieldbook: Strategies and Tools for Building a Learning Organization*. New York: Currency Doubleday.

Silos, L. 1991. OIKOS: *The Two Faces of Organization*. Manila: Asian Institute of Management.

Simons, R., and A. Dávila. 1998. *Harvard Business Review on Measuring Corporate Performance*. Cambridge, MA.: Harvard Business School Press.

Skinner, E. 1996. Traditional Institutions and Economic Development: The Mossi Nam. In A. Yansane (ed.), *Development Strategies in Africa: Current Economic, Socio-Political and Institutional Trends and Issues*. Greenwood Publishing Group.

Steers, R. 1975. Problems in the Measurement of Organizational Effectiveness. *Administrative Science Quarterly* (20): 546-48.

Stone, A., B. Levy, and R. Portes. 1996. Public Institutions and Private Transactions: A Comparative Analysis of the Legal and Regulatory Environment for Business Transactions in Brazil and Chile. In L.J. Alston, T. Eggertsson and D.C. North (eds.), *Empirical Studies in Institutional Change*. New York: Cambridge University Press.

Stoto, M.A. 1997. Research Synthesis for Public Health Policy: Experience of the Institute of Medicine. In E. Chelimsky and W.R. Shadish (eds.), *Evaluation for the 21st Century: A Handbook*. Thousand Oaks, CA: Sage.

Tavenas, F. 1992. *Performance Indicators at McGill*. Working Paper, McGill University, Montreal.

Taylor, F. 1998. *The Principles of Scientific Management*. New York: Dover.

Taylor, F. W. 1947. *Scientific Management*. New York: Harper and Row.

Tichy, N. 1997. *The Leadership Engine*. New York: Harper Business.

Tomassi, M., and A. Velasco. 1995. Where Are We in the Political Economy of Reform? Unpublished.

United Nations Development Programme (UNDP). 1993. *Human Development Report 1993*. New York: Oxford University Press.

University of British Columbia (UBC). 1998. Social Capital Formation and Institutions for Sustainability. Workshop, November 16-17, Vancouver, British Columbia. http://www.sdri.ubc.ca/gbfp/soc_cap.html

Uphoff, N. 1972. *The Political Economy of Development: Theoretical and Empirical Contributions*. Berkeley, CA.: University of California Press.

U.S. General Accounting Office. 1998. The Results Act: An Evaluator's Guide to Assessing Agency Annual Performance Plans. GAO General Goverment Division. April.

Vecchio, R. P. 1995. *Organizational Behaviour*. Orlando, FL.: Harcourt Brace and Co.

Walton, M. 1986. *The Deming Management Method*. New York: Putnam Publishing Group.

Weber, M. 1947. *The Theory of Social and Economic Organization*. New York: Free Press.

Weick, K. E. 1995. *Sensemaking in Organizations*. Thousand Oaks, CA: Sage.

Weisner, E. 1998. Transaction Cost Economics and Public Sector Rent Seeking in Developing Countries: Towards a Theory of Governance Failure. In R. Picciotto and E. Weisner (eds.), *Evaluation and Development: The Institutional Dimension*. Washington, D.C.: World Bank.

Wohlstetter, P. 1994. Models of High-Performance Schools. In S. A. Mohrman and P. Wohlstetter and Associates (eds.), *School-Based Management*. San Francisco: Jossey-Bass.

Yuchtman, E., and S. Seashore. 1967. Factorial Analysis of Organizational Performance. *Administrative Science Quarterly* 12(3): 377-95.

Zammuto, R. 1982. *Assessing Organizational Effectiveness: Systems Change, Adaptation and Strategy*. Albany, NY: SUNY Press.